ON MANAGEMENT **TAB EDWARDS**

ALSO BY TAB EDWARDS

MPS: Managed Print Services

The Art of Movement

Doing Your Job Successfully

Management By Initiatives

The 50-Hour Workweek in 20 Hours

Managing within a firm means skillfully harnessing every available resource—whether it's people, finances, knowledge, technology, or time—solely in pursuit of predefined objectives. Simultaneously, it's about fostering the prosperity and growth of those under the manager's guidance, ensuring that everyone in the reporting chain flourishes alongside the overarching goals.

You can't do anything without doing *something*.

A RESOURCE FOR PRACTICING MANAGERS

ON MANAGEMENT **TAB EDWARDS**

THE PERFORMANCE LABORATORY No 33 / TMBE MEDIA
PHILADELPHIA, PA. 19129

PHILADELPHIA, PA 19129

THE PERFORMANCE LABORATORY Nº 33 / TMBE MEDIA

Copyright © 2024 by Tab M. Edwards. All rights reserved.

Except as permitted under the United States Copyright Act of 1976, no part of this publication may be reproduced or distributed in any form or by any means, or stored in a data base or retrieval system, without the prior written permission of the publisher.

This publication is designed to provide authoritative information in regards to the subject matter covered. It is sold with the understanding that the publisher is not engaged in rendering legal, accounting, or other professional services. If legal advice or other expert assistance is required, the services of a competent professional person should be sought.

–From a declaration of principles jointly adopted by a committee of the American Bar Association and a committee of publishers.

Tab Edwards books are available at special quantity discounts to use as premiums and promotions, or for use in corporate training programs. For more information, please contact us at Info@TheLab33.com.

Designed by The Lab Creative
Philadelphia, PA.

1 3 5 7 9 10 8 6 4 2

TTX

CONTENTS

CONTENTS

PART ONE: PRINCIPLES

Introduction / The Manager	14
1 / Core Principles in Modern Management	40
2 / What Managers Do	52

PART TWO: TRANSITION

3 / From Competent to Exceptional	82
Five Management Practices for Excellence	87
I. Strategic planning and Execution	88
II. Manager Proficiency Assessment	126
III. Safety	137
IV. Performance Planning	141
V. Productivity	163
4 / The Management Journey	182
Conclusion	199
About the Author	203

PART ONE
PRINCIPLES

INTRODUCTION
THE MANAGER

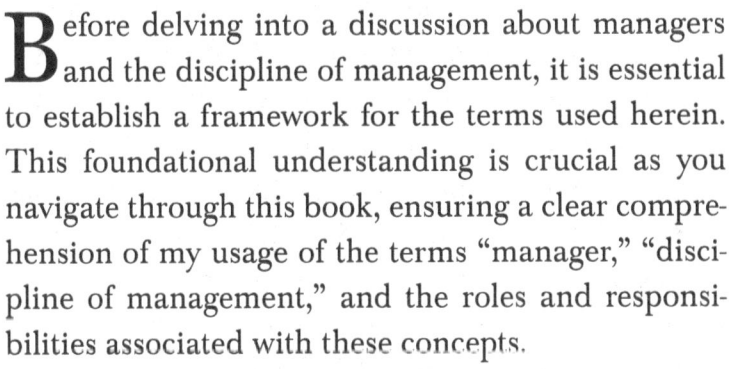

Before delving into a discussion about managers and the discipline of management, it is essential to establish a framework for the terms used herein. This foundational understanding is crucial as you navigate through this book, ensuring a clear comprehension of my usage of the terms "manager," "discipline of management," and the roles and responsibilities associated with these concepts.

As hard as it may be to believe, genuine uncertainty persists regarding what managers do for their organizations. One primary reason for this uncertainty is that each organizational structure implies (and, in a sense, dictates) specific functions and responsibilities for its management.

Organizations, in essence, cannot make decisions; it is the *people* within an organization who constitute its decision-making element. An organization does not exist outside of its people. The activities in which an organization engages are determined by people, traditionally in the form of *managers*. Managers serve a special function within organizations, holding decision-making and execution responsibilities.

The concept of a company manager began to emerge in the late 19th and early 20th centuries during the period of industrialization and the rise of large corporations. Before this time, most businesses were small, family-owned operations, and the owner was responsible for all aspects of the business, including management. However, as businesses grew larger and more complex, the need for specialized managers to oversee different aspects of the company arose.

One of the earliest and most influential management theorists was Frederick Taylor, considered the father of scientific management. In 1911, Taylor published "The Principles of Scientific Management," proposing that managers use scientific methods to study work processes and improve efficiency. His ideas were widely adopted by industrial managers, establishing the field of management as a distinct discipline.

Another important figure was Henri Fayol, a French industrialist and management theorist, who published his ideas in a book called "Administration

INTRODUCTION: THE MANAGER

Industrielle et Générale" in 1916. Fayol proposed that management was a separate function from ownership, and managers were responsible for planning, organizing, commanding, coordinating, and controlling the activities of the organization. His ideas were also widely adopted and laid the foundation for modern management practices.

Philosophically, managers within a business wield a multifaceted role, acting as orchestrators navigating the complex symphony of human dynamics, resources, and objectives. At their essence, they are *architects of harmony*, blending the aspirations of the organization with the capabilities of its individuals. They are the *guardians of vision*, translating lofty ideals into actionable steps and serving as conduits through which strategy finds its manifestation. Yet, their realm extends beyond strategy; they cultivate fertile grounds for growth, nurturing the talents within their team to blossom. Managers act as diplomats, mediating conflicts and fostering cohesion, crafting an environment where diverse voices harmonize. In essence, managers transcend titles; they are cultivators of potential, stewards of direction, and custodians of the delicate balance between ambition and reality within the dynamic tapestry of an organization.

The concept of a company manager began to emerge during the late 19th century and early 20th century due to the growth of large corporations and the need for specialized managers to oversee different aspects of the company. The work of management theorists like Frederick Taylor and Henri Fayol helped establish the field of management as a distinct discipline and laid the foundation for modern management practices.

The Discipline of Management:

Development of Management as a Discipline - Scientific Management

One of the most significant events with a lasting impact on modern business management is the development and widespread adoption of scientific management principles in the late 19th and early 20th centuries. Scientific management, also known as **Taylorism**, was a philosophy introduced by American engineer and manager Frederick Winslow Taylor. He aimed to improve industrial efficiency by applying the principles of scientific analysis to work processes and task design.

The main idea behind scientific management was to break down work processes into smaller, more efficient tasks and standardize these tasks to maximize productivity and efficiency. Taylor believed that, by using a scientific approach to management, workers could be trained to perform their tasks in the most efficient manner possible, leading to increased productivity and profitability for the company.

INTRODUCTION: THE MANAGER

Scientific management had a profound impact on the way businesses were managed and influenced the development of modern business management practices. Many of the principles of scientific management, such as the importance of standardization, efficient work processes, and the use of data and analytics to improve performance, are still widely used today. In addition, the emphasis on worker training and development and the recognition of the importance of human resources management can also be traced back to the principles of scientific management.

In the world of business and organizational dynamics, the term "discipline" within the context of management encapsulates a structured framework of principles, methodologies, and practices that collectively steer the course of effective leadership and operational success. It embodies a systematic approach to orchestrating resources and encompasses adherence to established principles, best practices, and ethical standards while guiding teams and navigating the complexities of the business landscape toward strategic goals and predetermined objectives.

The discipline of management stands as a cornerstone in the domain of business, continually evolving to meet the dynamic challenges of the corporate landscape. Esteemed institutions like Harvard Business School and renowned consulting firms such as McKinsey & Company have contributed seminal insights that shape the discipline, understanding, and practice of effective management, as has American social psychologist and renowned management thinker Douglas McGregor.

Harvard Business School, a venerated institution in business education, defines management as the art of coordinating resources and people to achieve organizational objectives. Their insights emphasize the importance of strategic thinking, leadership, and adaptability in steering organizations through turbulent markets and rapid technological advancements. McKinsey & Company, a globally esteemed management consultancy, emphasizes strategic management as a *linchpin for sustainable growth*. Their thought leadership highlights the significance of innovation, agility, and data-driven decision-making in achieving competitive advantage and market resilience.

McGregor, through his influential work, particularly his *Theory X* and *Theory Y*, presented contrasting views on how managers perceive and interact with their employees. His theories fundamentally shape how management is understood in terms of the assumptions managers hold about their employees' motivations and behaviors. McGregor's Theory X suggests that managers who adhere to certain assumptions believe that employees inherently dislike work, avoid responsibility, and *need to be controlled and coerced* to achieve organizational goals. Managers following this view often employ strict supervision, hier-

INTRODUCTION: THE MANAGER

archical structures, and punishment/reward systems to motivate employees.

On the other hand, Theory Y proposes a contrasting perspective where managers assume that employees are *inherently motivated*, enjoy work, seek responsibility, and can be self-directed and creative in achieving organizational objectives. Managers following this theory tend to empower employees, encourage participation, and create opportunities for growth and self-fulfillment at work.

I believe that a disciplined approach within management involves three things:

A Structural Framework: Management discipline provides a structured framework encompassing strategic planning, resource allocation, decision-making processes, and operational execution.

Consistency and Rigor: It emphasizes consistency in processes, rigor in methodologies, and adherence to established ethical norms and standards, ensuring a systematic and organized approach to management practices.

Adaptability and Continual Improvement: While embracing structure, management discipline also allows for adaptability and continual improvement, enabling organizations to respond to changes, innovate, and evolve with the dynamic business landscape.

So, what is a manager?

What is a Manager?

Becoming a manager can occur in various ways, even without an official title. This can happen informally, based on the qualities, activities, and responsibilities assumed by the person, or their leadership abilities and job proficiency. It can also occur formally, when leaders in the organization confer the title of "manager" upon an individual.

For instance, if I join a firm and, due to having the most practical experience in my department, the boss designates me as the project leader for a team of less experienced workers to enhance the project's chances of success. As time progresses, the project is delivered with excellence. The boss, gaining more confidence in my abilities and leadership, entrusts me with leading the entire department to help develop the less experienced staff and ensure our collective success. Additionally, the boss links one of my Key Performance Indicators (KPI) to the department's success in achieving revenue targets, implying that I now have a degree of accountability for the department's performance. Effectively, this would make me a de facto department *manager*, even though I was not officially assigned the formal title in my job description.

The other, more traditional way that a person becomes a manager is simply by being given the formal title in the person's employment agreement. Even

INTRODUCTION: THE MANAGER

if the person is fresh out of college, has no practical experience, has never managed anything, but is the boss's nephew and has been given a job with the title of "Manager," that person, by virtue of holding that job title, will be considered a manager.

> **Even if the person is fresh out of college, has no practical experience, has never managed anything, but is the boss's nephew and has been given a job with the title of "Manager," that person, by virtue of holding that job title, will be considered a manager.**

While these are the most common ways a person can effectively become a manager, the two scenarios illustrate a management truism: just because a person holds the title of "manager," it does not mean they know how to *manage* (more on that later) or are any good at it. It just means that, according to their Human Resources file, they are officially a manager.

Whether a person is a de facto manager or formally holds the title, there are several **requirements that an individual must meet** to be considered a manager in an organization.

- *Authority*: A manager must have the authority to make decisions and give directions to others. This authority is typically given by the organization's leadership and is often formalized through a job title, such as "manager" or "supervisor."

- *Responsibility*: A manager must be responsible for the performance of a specific group of individuals, such as a team or department. They are responsible for the performance and output of their team or department, and they are accountable for any issues that arise.

- *Knowledge*: A manager should have knowledge and understanding of the business and industry in which their organization operates. They should also have knowledge of the functions and processes that are specific to their team or department.

- *Leadership*: A manager must be able to lead and inspire others. They must be able to communicate their vision, set goals, and provide guidance to their team.

- *Communication Effectiveness*: A manager should be able to communicate effectively with their team, other managers, and other stakeholders within the organization. They should be able to convey information clearly and accurately and should be able to listen actively and respond appropriately to feedback.

INTRODUCTION: THE MANAGER

- *Problem-Solving Ability*: A manager should be able to analyze and solve problems to improve the performance of their team or department.

Becoming a manager is not just about a title; it's about influencing and leading others effectively. Your actions, attitude, and contributions can position you as a de facto manager, even without the formal designation.

At Their Core, What Do Managers Do?

It varies

When asked, generally, "What do managers do?", most people will provide a list of activities and responsibilities that someone in the manager role should do. For example, Adam Smith, often considered the father of modern economics for his foundational work in the field, would likely explain the role of managers in a firm through the lens of their economic function. In his view, managers play a crucial role as coordinators of labor and resources. They act as catalysts for efficiency and productivity within an organization by allocating resources judiciously and directing the efforts of individuals toward common goals. Smith would see managers as essential components in the division of labor, ensuring that each part contributes effectively to the overall operation of the business. Their role, in Smith's eyes, would encompass overseeing the organization's functions, optimizing processes, and facilitating the smooth flow of operations to enhance both productivity and profitability. Their primary function would be to efficiently organize and direct the efforts of individuals to maximize productivity and output.

Smith might emphasize that managers serve as facilitators, ensuring that each worker's skills and efforts are directed towards the most effective and productive ends. They allocate resources, delegate responsibilities, and supervise operations to streamline the production process, thus contributing to the overall success and efficiency of the firm. Additionally, managers, according to Smith, would play a crucial role in maintaining discipline and order within the workforce, ensuring adherence to established procedures and standards, ultimately contributing to the firm's competitiveness and success in the market.

Again, this is a list of things a manager *should do*, not actually what they *do*.

The discussion of what a person performing the role of a manager does versus what they should do is a core concept of this book. Extensive research conducted by the Performance Laboratory No. 33, Marketing & Business Integration, and The Water Group consultancy sheds light on the types of activities in which *people-managers*—managers or supervisors responsible for overseeing and leading a team or a

INTRODUCTION: THE MANAGER

group of individuals within an organization—hereinafter referred to as "managers," most consistently engage.

It is worth noting that managers within a firm are not a monolith: a uniform or homogenous group. There is diversity and individuality among managers in terms of their experience, skills, approaches, styles, and beliefs about management. Through our research, we have identified six different types and levels of managers based on their experience and proficiency in the role. Our findings show that managers at different experience and proficiency levels behave differently and consistently perform different activities with varying degrees of effectiveness. For example, a first-time manager working at a small business who has not had advanced training and no track record of success as a manager would perform the job differently and engage in different activities than would a 20-year, successful, seasoned veteran working at IBM.

"Their primary function would be to efficiently organize and direct the efforts of individuals to maximize productivity and output." -Adam Smith

DEFINITIONS

Management Experience

This refers to the duration and depth of a person's involvement in managerial roles or positions. It includes the time spent managing teams, projects, departments, or entire organizations. Management experience can encompass various aspects such as leading teams, making strategic decisions, handling conflicts, overseeing operations, and being accountable for achieving goals. It's not solely about the time spent in a managerial role but also the range and complexity of challenges faced and addressed during that time.

Management Proficiency

This relates to the level of skill, expertise, and competence an individual possesses in performing managerial tasks and responsibilities. It includes the ability to effectively plan, organize, lead, and control resources to achieve organizational objectives. Proficiency in management involves a combination of knowledge, practical skills, leadership qualities, and the capability to navigate various managerial situations effectively. It's about how well someone can execute managerial duties and make decisions that positively impact their team and the organization.

Management Effectiveness

This measures the degree to which a manager successfully achieves desired outcomes and objectives in their managerial role. Effectiveness in management involves accomplishing goals efficiently, leading a team towards success, meeting performance metrics, fostering a productive work environment, and contributing to the overall success of the organization. It's about the tangible results and impact a manager has on their team and the broader organizational goals.

INTRODUCTION: THE MANAGER

I believe it is not constructive to talk about managers as though they perform the job the same and are all equal; they are not. Treating them as such would prove useless for trying to understand how to become a better manager based on where one might be on the experience curve. For this reason, we created a table delineating the various levels of the manager role based on experience, proficiency, and effectiveness. This is illustrated in the table below.

Management Hierarchy

VARIOUS LEVELS OF MANAGER*
Management Development /Non-People Manager
This refers to the duration and depth of a person's involvement in managerial roles or positions. It includes the time spent managing teams, projects, departments, or entire organizations. Management experience can encompass various aspects such as leading teams, making strategic decisions, handling
New Manager / Entry Level
These are individuals who have recently transitioned into managerial positions, often overseeing small teams or specific tasks within a department. They might have titles like team leader, supervisor, or junior manager.
Mid-Level Manager
Positioned between entry-level and senior management, mid-level managers supervise larger teams or entire departments. Titles might include department manager, division head, or regional manager.

VARIOUS LEVELS OF MANAGER*
Experienced Manager
With more tenure and expertise, experienced managers might oversee multiple departments or complex projects. They might hold titles like senior manager, director, or senior director.
Executive Manager
This tier includes top-level executives responsible for strategic decision-making and overseeing the organization as a whole. Titles here often include C-suite positions such as CEO (Chief Executive Officer), COO (Chief Operating Officer), CFO (Chief Financial Officer), and CMO (Chief Marketing Officer).
Senior Leadership / Board Level Manager
In larger corporations or organizations, there might be additional layers between executive management and the board level, such as Vice Presidents (VPs) or Senior Vice Presidents (SVPs) who oversee specific areas or divisions.

* The specific titles and number of managerial levels can differ significantly between industries, companies, and organizational structures. Smaller companies might have fewer managerial tiers, while larger corporations might have more complex hierarchies with numerous managerial levels in between. Additionally, some organizations might have specialized managerial roles such as project managers, product managers, or functional managers, which might exist across various hierarchical levels based on their scope of responsibility.

INTRODUCTION: THE MANAGER

The activities in which managers engage will vary depending on their level and role within the management hierarchy and their position on the **Manager Experience Curve**.

The experience curve generally illustrates the relationship between experience (often measured in time and growth) and effectiveness in a role. In the context of managers, it showcases how their effectiveness tends to increase with more experience, training, and knowledge.

The Y-axis represents effectiveness, indicating how well a manager performs in their role, while the X-axis represents experience, often measured in years or increments of time.

The curve typically starts relatively low on the Y-axis when a manager begins their role, indicating lower effectiveness due to being new and having limited experience or knowledge. As time progresses along the X-axis, the curve tends to rise, showing an upward trend in effectiveness. This rise signifies that as managers gain more valuable experiences, they become more effective in their roles.

THE MANAGER EXPERIENCE CURVE

THIS IMPACT REFLECTS THE ABILITY TO ABSORB AND GAIN VALUE FROM THESE EXPERIENCES

The Performance Lab No 33

| TRAINING & EDUCATION | ON THE JOB EXPERIENCES | MISTAKES & ADAPTABILITY | OBSERVATION, LEARNING FROM OTHERS | MENTORSHIP & FEEDBACK | TENURE & SUCCESS |

NEW MANAGER ──────── INTERNALIZED EXPERIENCES ──────── SENIOR LEADER

EFFECTIVENESS

INTRODUCTION: THE MANAGER

As this graphic illustrates, emerging and new managers often lack significant experience in the role and, therefore, strive to learn the job and become better at it. Conversely, more experienced managers have had varied experiences—including valuable failures—that have helped them become highly effective in the job.

New managers generally focus on learning and development and observation to become acclimated to the job, whereas experienced managers focus more on mentoring, self-reflection, the value of gaining successes, and strategy execution.

What is interesting to note about the experience arc through which managers navigate in the job is how, after so many years performing managerial roles, most managers become stale, less motivated, and less effective.

As depicted, the manager's growth, development, and effectiveness are not linear, increasing at an increasing rate over time for as long as the person occupies the job. The arc or curve is more mountainous in form. As the manager internalizes the value that various experiences offer, our study shows that their effectiveness will, at best, increase, however at a decreasing rate over time.

At a macro level, the methods or approaches through which managers acquire skills and qualities that contribute to their effectiveness include:

- *Training and Development:* This involves formal programs, workshops, courses, or seminars specifically designed to enhance managerial skills. Leadership training programs, management workshops, or professional development courses offer targeted learning experiences.
- *Leadership Training:* Specific training focused on developing leadership skills. These programs often cover topics like communication, decision-making, team management, and strategic thinking tailored to foster effective leadership qualities.
- *On-the-Job Experience:* Managers learn through practical experience gained by performing managerial tasks, handling challenges, and leading teams within their role. This hands-on experience helps them apply theoretical knowledge in real-world situations.
- *Learning from Experience:* Reflecting on and learning from past experiences, both successes and failures, contribute significantly to a manager's growth. Analyzing what worked well and what didn't helps in refining managerial approaches.
- *Mentorship and Role Models:* Having mentors or role models provides guidance, advice, and insights into effective managerial practices. Learning from experienced individuals helps in developing managerial skills and navigating challenges.

- *Practice and Feedback:* Managers improve their skills through continuous practice and receive feedback from peers, superiors, or team members. Constructive feedback allows them to identify areas for improvement and refine their managerial abilities.
- *Observation and Learning from Others:* Managers observe successful leaders, colleagues, or industry experts, studying their approaches and adopting effective strategies they witness. This observational learning contributes to skill development.
- *Self-Reflection and Awareness:* Engaging in self-reflection, assessing strengths, weaknesses, and behaviors, enhances self-awareness. This introspection aids in understanding one's impact as a manager and areas needing improvement.

Broadly, this is what managers do. While these factors are key contributors to managerial effectiveness, it is essential to recognize that successful management often involves a combination of various skills and qualities. Adaptability, decision-making abilities, strategic thinking, and continuous learning also play significant roles in shaping an effective manager. Additionally, the specific context of the industry, organizational culture, and the managerial role itself can influence which factors are most crucial for success. As we assess these factors in greater detail, we will explore, at a more granular level, the skills and qualities that directly contribute to managerial effectiveness.

Value Delivery

Not all managers contribute equally. As I discussed in the book "MBI: Management By Initiatives," a firm's strategic focus is twofold: at the organization level, the focus is on delivering value, while at the business unit level, the focus is on creating a sustainable competitive advantage. Managers at different stages within an organization—new managers, mid-level managers, experienced managers, and executive managers—deliver different levels of value to the organization.

As one would expect, new managers work more tactically and deliver little strategic value and lower levels of competitive advantage than their more proficient counterparts. Conversely, executive managers deliver significant strategic value and lay the foundation for competitive value delivery at the business unit level. This is represented in the quadrant diagram below, depicting the elements of value delivery, competitive advantage, and the balance between tactical and strategic focus for the four types of managers.

The diagram plots the previously mentioned four types of managers along two axes: Delivery of Value (ranging from operational/execution-focused to strategic/visionary) and Tactical vs. Strategic inclination (from tactical-oriented to strategic-oriented). Each manager type is placed in a quadrant according to

INTRODUCTION: THE MANAGER

their position on these axes, visually representing their typical focus on value delivery and their inclination towards tactical or strategic approaches to management.

This diagram provides a snapshot view of how different types of managers approach their roles in terms of value delivery and strategic thinking, allowing for comparisons and insights into their typical managerial approaches.

	HIGHLY TACTICAL	HIGHLY STRATEGIC
HIGH VALUE & COMPETITIVE ADVANTAGE		EXECUTIVE MANAGER
		EXPERIENCED MANAGER
LOW VALUE & COMPETITIVE DISADVANTAGE	MID-LEVEL MANAGER	
	NEW MANAGER	

New Manager:

- *Delivery of Value*: Typically more focused on immediate tasks and learning the ropes. They contribute value by executing tasks efficiently and learning from experiences.

- *Tactical vs. Strategic*: Tends to lean more towards the tactical side initially, prioritizing day-to-day operations and immediate goals over long-term strategy.

Mid-level Manager:

- *Delivery of Value*: Balances execution with some strategic thinking. They add value by ensuring team efficiency, improving processes, and contributing to mid-term objectives.
- *Tactical vs. Strategic*: Likely to balance both aspects, engaging in both tactical execution and beginning to contribute strategically to achieve mid-term goals.

Experienced Manager:

- *Delivery of Value*: Brings a blend of strategic vision and effective execution. Their value lies in aligning team efforts with long-term goals, driving innovation, and optimizing processes.
- *Tactical vs. Strategic*: Skews more towards the strategic side, focusing on long-term planning, innovation, and guiding the team towards broader organizational objectives.

Executive Manager:

- *Delivery of Value*: Primarily focused on strategic direction, vision, and ensuring alignment with the organization's overall goals. They provide value through setting high-level strategies and shaping the organizational culture.
- *Tactical vs. Strategic*: Primarily strategic, concentrating on setting the overall direction, long-term planning, and securing competitive advantage for the organization.

INTRODUCTION: THE MANAGER

Now that we have established a framework for the levels of management, their broad behaviors, and the value they deliver to organizations, we are better equipped to discuss the universal and timeless core principles of management in the modern age.

CHAPTER ONE
CORE PRINCIPLES IN MODERN MANAGEMENT

1

At The Performance Laboratory No 33 (The Lab), we believe that the "core principles" of modern management encompass foundational concepts that serve as guiding beliefs or philosophies essential for effective managerial practice. These principles are fundamental doctrines that underpin successful managerial approaches, emphasizing their universal applicability and enduring significance across industries and organizational contexts. The nature of a "core" principle lies in its inherent **universality and timelessness**, forming the bedrock of managerial thought and action. These principles are not fleeting trends but enduring truths that shape managerial strategies, decision-making, and leadership practices. Their significance extends beyond immediate trends or industry-specific practices, offering enduring wisdom adaptable to evolving business landscapes.

The positive impact of core principles on managers is multifaceted. They provide a framework for decision-making, guiding managers in navigating complex challenges, fostering organizational growth, and achieving sustainable success. These principles equip managers with a compass to steer through uncertainty, aligning their actions with overarching goals and values. Additionally, they aid in establishing a cohesive organizational culture, nurturing a sense of direction, accountability, and collaboration among team members. Embracing these principles empowers managers to create environments conducive to innovation, adaptability, and employee engagement, driving overall organizational effectiveness.

What is surprising to many is that, we believe, there are only a handful of managerial principles that we consider to be core to the success of anyone performing the manager's job. Core principles of modern management encompass a few fundamental concepts, including:

- **Strategic Alignment**
- **Ethical Leadership**
- **Continuous Improvement**
- **Empowerment and Collaboration**

CORE PRINCIPLES IN MODERN MANAGEMENT

STRATEGIC ALIGNMENT

Ensuring that all managerial actions and decisions align with the organization's strategic objectives. This principle emphasizes the importance of clarity in goals and direction, guiding managers to make choices that contribute to the organization's long-term success. It ensures that every level of the organization, from individual teams to departments, works cohesively towards the same strategic goals.

Example: An example of strategic alignment is when a company's marketing department aligns its campaigns with the broader corporate strategy to expand into new markets. Every marketing effort and initiative is aimed at supporting the company's expansion goals.	**Necessity for Effective Management:** Strategic alignment is crucial as it provides clarity, direction, and a unified focus within the organization. It enables efficient resource allocation, minimizes conflicting objectives, and enhances organizational agility by ensuring that all efforts are directed towards common strategic outcomes.

ETHICAL LEADERSHIP

Upholding ethical standards and integrity in all managerial practices. Ethical leadership involves making decisions that consider the impact on stakeholders, fostering trust, and maintaining transparency in actions and communications.

Example: A CEO who prioritizes fair treatment of employees, transparency in business practices, and environmentally responsible operations demonstrates ethical leadership. They make decisions considering the ethical implications beyond immediate profitability.	**Necessity for Effective Management:** Ethical leadership fosters trust, credibility, and a positive organizational culture. It establishes a foundation of integrity, guiding ethical decision-making and behavior within the organization, ultimately enhancing reputation and long-term sustainability.

CONTINUOUS IMPROVEMENT

Encouraging a culture of continuous learning, innovation, and adaptation. This principle involves seeking opportunities for growth, embracing change, and fostering a mindset of ongoing improvement at both individual and organizational levels.

Example: A manufacturing company implements a Kaizen approach, encouraging employees to suggest and implement small, incremental improvements in processes regularly. This leads to increased efficiency and quality over time.

Necessity for Effective Management: Continuous improvement is vital for staying competitive and adapting to changing market conditions. It fosters innovation, efficiency, and adaptability, enabling organizations to evolve, grow, and remain relevant in dynamic business environments.

EMPOWERMENT & COLLABORATION

Empowering and involving employees in decision-making processes, fostering collaboration, and leveraging diverse perspectives and talents within the team. This principle promotes a culture of inclusivity and harnesses collective strengths.

Example: A manager empowers their team by providing them with the authority to make decisions within their scope. They encourage cross-departmental collaboration, allowing diverse perspectives to contribute to innovative solutions.

Necessity for Effective Management: Empowerment and collaboration drive employee engagement, creativity, and a sense of ownership. They promote a culture of innovation, improve problem-solving capabilities, and enhance productivity by leveraging diverse skills and knowledge within the organization.

Acquiring these core principles involves a multifaceted approach. They are cultivated through a combination of education, experience, mentorship, and intentional practice. Formal education in management provides foundational knowledge, exposing aspiring managers to these principles and their application in various contexts. Practical experience, including exposure to real-world managerial challenges, offers opportunities to apply these principles and learn from successes and failures. Additionally, mentorship from seasoned leaders or role models provides valuable insights and guidance in embracing these principles, while continuous reflection and self-assessment contribute to their internalization. Ultimately, the integration of these principles into managerial practice is an ongoing journey, requiring a commitment to lifelong learning and a dedication to embodying these principles in everyday managerial actions.

Adapting Modern Management Principles to Conemporary Realities

To reiterate, *core principles* are not fleeting fads but *enduring truths* that shape managerial strategies, decision-making, and leadership practices. If one is to manage effectively, their thoughts and actions should be driven by these enduring principles: Strategic Alignment, Ethical Leadership, Continuous Improvement, and Empowerment and Collaboration.

Although we believe these core principles should be at the heart of managerial practice, we cannot ignore the realities of technological advances, the ever-changing global environment, evolving employee work models, new learnings in the management discipline, and multifaceted workforces. It is like baking a pound cake.

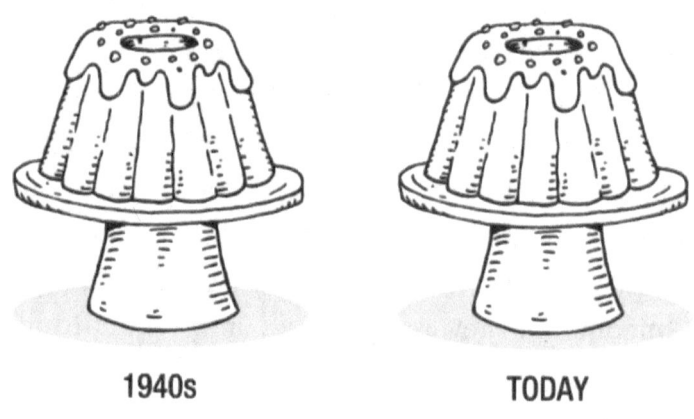

1940s   TODAY

In the 1940s, a traditional pound cake—so named because, historically, it referred to a cake made with a *pound* each of flour, butter, sugar, and eggs—typically included these basic pantry staples commonly available during that time: flour, butter, sugar, eggs, a leavening agent (e.g., baking powder), vanilla extract, and milk. Mix them together and bake it in the oven at about 350°F. These were the core principles for baking a pound cake in the 1940s; universal and timeless. Today, they remain the core principles for baking a pound cake. However, with technological advancements, evolved cooking techniques, and available ingredients, bakers have *adapted modern cake-baking principles to contemporary realities.*

Technologically, modern ovens have precise temperature controls, convection settings, and even heat distribution, ensuring more consistent baking results compared to older ovens. Advanced stand mixers, hand mixers, and other kitchen tools offer improved efficiency and convenience, allowing for faster and more thorough mixing, beating, and blending.

Improved ingredient quality and availability have made it possible to turn out an even tastier, higher quality cake. For example, flour quality has improved, offering more refined options, and leavening agents like baking powder and baking soda are now more reliable and readily available. Plus, quality control in dairy production ensures better butter and milk consistency, and eggs are often larger and more consistent in size, providing better structure and moisture to the cake.

Cooking techniques and recipes have also evolved, resulting in variations of pound cake, from traditional recipes to gluten-free, vegan, or healthier versions. Access to online resources, cooking shows, and cookbooks provides a wealth of information, allowing aspiring bakers to experiment with various techniques and recipes.

So, while the core principles are necessary for producing a great pound cake, adapting to contemporary realities has enabled bakers to take their results to higher levels. The same concept holds true for core management principles and the value of adapting these principles to contemporary realities.

> **So, while the core principles are necessary for producing a great pound cake, adapting to contemporary realities has enabled bakers to take their results to higher levels. The same concept holds true for core management principles and the value of adapting these principles to contemporary realities.**

Contemporary managerial practice faces a landscape shaped by rapid technological advancements, dynamic global environments, evolving work models, and multifaceted workforces. While core principles like Strategic Alignment, Ethical Leadership, Continuous Improvement, and Empowerment and Collaboration remain crucial, acknowledging the impact of modern realities is essential. This discussion explores the evolving nature of management principles and introduces four key adaptations necessitated by the current landscape.

Strategic Vision and Leadership

- *Adaptation:* In the face of evolving global environments and technological disruptions, strategic vision and leadership have expanded. Leaders must now possess foresight to anticipate market shifts, embrace innovation, and pivot strategies swiftly.

- *Rationale:* The accelerated pace of technological advancements demands leaders who can envision long-term strategies while being agile enough to adapt to rapidly changing circumstances.

Agility and Adaptability

- *Adaptation:* The traditional emphasis on static strategic plans has shifted towards agility and adaptability. Organizations prioritize flexible frameworks that allow quick response to market changes or emerging opportunities.

- *Rationale:* With the unpredictability of global markets and work environments, the ability to swiftly pivot strategies, structures, and operations becomes a competitive advantage.

Data-Informed Decision-Making

- *Adaptation:* Technological advancements have propelled the importance of data-informed decision-making. Managers now rely on real-time analytics, AI-driven insights, and big data to make informed and agile decisions.

- *Rationale*: In a data-driven world, harnessing analytics provides managers with accurate, timely information crucial for strategic choices and resource allocation.

Talent Management and Development:

- *Adaptation*: Multifaceted workforces demand a shift in talent management. Modern managers focus on fostering inclusivity, promoting diversity, and tailoring development programs to accommodate diverse skill sets and remote work models.

- *Rationale*: The evolving workforce composition necessitates adaptive talent strategies to attract, retain, and develop diverse talents contributing to innovation and organizational growth.

While core principles of management remain invaluable, adapting these principles to current realities is imperative for organizational success. Strategic Vision and Leadership, Agility and Adaptability, Data-Informed Decision-Making, and Talent Management and Development are critical adaptations in response to technological advancements, global changes, evolving work models, and diverse workforces. Embracing these adaptations equips managers to navigate the complexities of the modern landscape, fostering resilience, innovation, and sustainable growth in today's dynamic business environment.

CORE PRINCIPLES IN MODERN MANAGEMENT

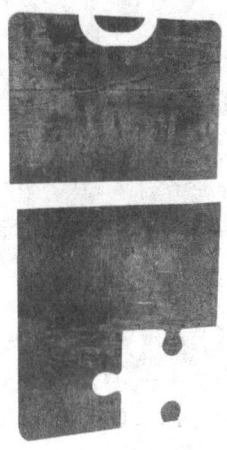

CHAPTER TWO
WHAT MANAGERS DO

MANAGER RESPONSIBILITIES

What a "manager" *is* can best be described by the responsibilities of someone holding that job or title. Simplistically, a manager can be described as a person with the authority to decide on key issues while considering the structure, function, and "needs" of the market in which the organization does business.

Managers develop and manage people (ultimately being held accountable for their subordinates' decisions and activities), build coalitions, allocate resources, and decide upon go-forward actions. Simultaneously, the manager is a figurehead, representative, information disseminator, and networker. To quote Henry Mintzberg, a well-known management scholar and author of the 1973 book "The Nature of Managerial Work," "Managing is about helping organizations and units to get things done, which means action."

I am in absolute agreement that managers' primary focus should be on *accomplishment*, defined as the achievement of business-unit and organizational objectives manifested in strategy initiatives. To accomplish something means to bring it to its *goal*, to achieve a defined and necessary end. Isn't this what managers are ultimately hired to do? Managers should always be mindful of their purpose within the organization and focus on achieving the goals and objectives—the necessary *ends*—they are charged with, rather than simply engaging in unrelated activities and day-to-day busy work. Without guidance, individuals will do the things they think are important, often resulting in uncoordinated, divergent, even conflicting decisions and actions. Any activity in which a manager engages that does not directly support organizational goals is a wasted effort.

> **Any activity in which a manager engages that does not directly support organizational goals is a wasted effort.**

It should be clear that managers play a critical role in the success of a company—excluding cases where the "manager" is merely a *zero-impact* figurehead. Managers are responsible for setting goals and objectives, creating and implementing plans, and allocating resources to help the company achieve its objectives. They also oversee the work of employees and ensure that they are meeting their job responsibilities. To effectively perform the various activities of developing and managing people, deciding upon go-forward actions, disseminating information, and networking, among others, managers benefit greatly by enhancing certain skills.

Managers must have strong leadership and communication skills to effectively motivate and guide their employees. They must also be able to make difficult decisions and solve problems, as well as be knowledgeable in their area of expertise. Additionally, they are responsible for managing the financial and operational aspects of the company, including budgeting, forecasting, and monitoring performance metrics, depending on the organization's needs and job description requirements.

A manager's role as an information disseminator involves communicating and distributing important information throughout the organization. This can include updates on company performance, changes in policies and procedures, and new initiatives or projects. It's essential for the manager to have a clear understanding of the information they are communicating and to present it in a clear and concise manner that is easily understood by employees. This helps ensure that everyone is on the same page, and that the organization is operating in a coordinated and efficient manner.

In addition to disseminating information, a manager's role as a relationship builder involves creating and maintaining strong relationships with employees, customers, and other stakeholders. This requires effective communication skills, empathy, and a genuine interest in the well-being of others. Managers must be able to understand the perspectives and needs of different groups and work collaboratively with them to achieve common goals. They must also be able to manage conflicts and resolve disputes in a fair and constructive manner.

Building positive relationships with employees is critical for a manager's success, as it contributes to a supportive and productive work environment. When employees feel valued and supported, they are more likely to be engaged and motivated, leading to increased job satisfaction and improved performance. Strong relationships with customers and other stakeholders are also essential for the success of the organization, as they help build trust and credibility and can lead to increased sales and revenue.

A manager's role in building contacts and networking involves establishing and maintaining relationships with individuals and organizations that can benefit the company. This can involve building relationships with customers, suppliers, industry experts, and other professionals. By establishing a network of contacts, a manager can access valuable information, resources, and opportunities that can help improve the company's performance and achieve its goals.

To be effective in building contacts and networking, a manager must have strong communication skills, be personable and approachable, and be able to establish **trust and credibility** with others. They must also be able to identify the key individuals and organizations that can benefit the company and actively seek out opportunities to meet and connect with them. This can involve attending industry events, participating in professional organizations, and leveraging social media and other online tools.

In addition to building new relationships, a manager must also work to maintain existing relationships by staying in touch with key contacts and keeping them informed of the company's activities and developments. This can involve regular email or phone communication and can also involve meeting with contacts in person to discuss potential opportunities and to build deeper relationships.

Networking and building contacts can also help a manager stay informed about industry trends, emerging technologies, and other important developments that can impact the company. By maintaining a network of contacts, a manager can gain valuable insights into the market and access new ideas and opportunities that can help drive the company's success.

A manager is responsible for overseeing the work of a team or department and ensuring that tasks are completed efficiently and effectively. They also play a vital role in setting goals and strategies for the organization and ensuring that these goals are met.

One of the most important responsibilities of a manager is to lead and motivate their team. A good manager should be able to effectively communicate the company's goals and objectives and ensure that their team members understand **how their work contributes to the overall success of the organization**. They should also be able to provide feedback and recognition for a job well done and provide support and guidance when necessary.

Another key responsibility of a manager is to make important decisions that will impact the organization. This includes decisions related to budgeting, staffing, and resource allocation. A manager must be able to analyze data and information and make informed decisions based on this information. They must also be able to anticipate and respond to changes in the marketplace and make adjustments to the organization's strategies as necessary.

Managers also play a critical role in developing and maintaining relationships with key stakeholders, such as customers, suppliers, and investors. They must be able to effectively communicate the organization's vision and goals and build trust and loyalty with these stakeholders. This is essential for the long-term success of the organization.

To summarize, a manager plays a crucial role in leading and directing the work of a team or department. They are responsible for setting goals and objectives, creating plans to achieve them, and ensuring that the team has the resources and support they need to be successful. Managers also act as a liaison between the team and upper management, communicating progress and addressing any issues that arise. Additionally, they are responsible for hiring, training, and evaluating team members, as well as motivating and inspiring them to reach their full potential. Overall, the role of a manager is to ensure the smooth operation and success of the team or department they oversee.

> **Managers are responsible for setting goals and objectives, creating plans to achieve them, and ensuring that the team has the resources and support they need to be successful.**

To perform optimally in the role, the manager must possess a wide range of skills, not just those described in the paragraphs above, but also the modern management and core principles, including strategic alignment, ethical leadership, continuous improvement, and empowerment and collaboration.

In the chapters that follow, we will dissect the specific activities in which a manager engages, from the formulation of strategic objectives to the daily intricacies of team leadership. By first scrutinizing the core principles, discussing the importance of embracing contemporary management philosophies, and unraveling the overarching general management responsibilities as we have done, I aim to paint a comprehensive picture of the multifaceted and dynamic role that managers play in the modern organization.

THE TRIAD OF MANAGEMENT

Principles, Responsibilities, and Activities

Effective management is a multifaceted endeavor that requires the discipline of working within an adaptable framework and a nuanced understanding of key elements of proficiency, namely management principles, responsibilities, and activities.

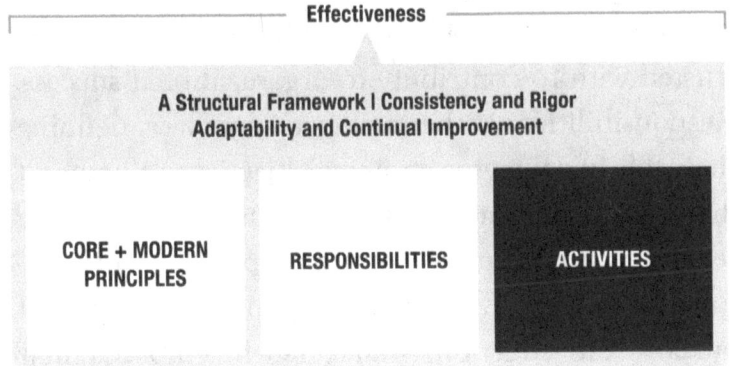

These elements form an interconnected triad, each contributing uniquely to the achievement of organizational objectives. Managers who navigate these components adeptly, balancing philosophical underpinnings with strategic responsibilities and tangible actions, are better positioned to lead teams toward success in today's dynamic business landscape.

Recognizing how the interplay of management principles, responsibilities, and activities will influence your efficacy as a manager holds significant importance. Management principles serve as the bedrock upon which managerial decisions are made. These are universal guidelines that transcend industry boundaries and provide a framework for effective leadership. Principles such as unity of command, delegation, and equity establish the philosophical underpinnings of management. They act as guiding lights, shaping the manager's approach to problem-solving, decision-making, and overall strategic direction.

Management responsibilities encapsulate the overarching duties and obligations that managers are entrusted with to contribute to organizational success. Responsibilities set the manager's compass, defining their role in achieving strategic objectives. Whether it involves formulating a vision for the team, ensuring resource allocation, or fostering a positive work culture, these high-level expectations provide a sense of purpose and direction. Managers who embrace their responsibilities with clarity contribute significantly to the attainment of broader organizational goals.

While principles and responsibilities provide the framework and strategic direction, management activities constitute the practical, day-to-day manifestations of a manager's role; it is where managers translate intent into action and planning into doing. Activities are the tangible actions that managers undertake to fulfill their responsibilities. Whether it's planning, organizing, communicating, or problem-solving, these concrete tasks are the building blocks of managerial effectiveness. Activities are the means through which principles are applied, and responsibilities are actualized. Successful managers navigate these activities with agility and precision, ensuring that their actions align with organizational objectives.

> **While principles and responsibilities provide the framework and strategic direction, management activities constitute the practical, day-to-day manifestations of a manager's role; it is where managers translate intent into action and planning to doing.**

The Critical Interplay

The synergy between management principles, responsibilities, and activities is paramount for success in the managerial role. Management principles guide decision-making, ensuring that choices align with established philosophies. Responsibilities provide a sense of purpose, directing managerial efforts toward strategic goals. Activities, in turn, translate these principles and responsibilities into tangible outcomes, fostering operational efficiency and effectiveness. These elements form an interconnected triad, each contributing uniquely to the achievement of organizational objectives. Managers who navigate these components adeptly, balancing philosophical underpinnings with strategic responsibilities and tangible actions, are better positioned to lead teams toward success in today's dynamic business landscape. However, while guiding principles and necessary responsibilities have proven to be invaluable for managerial success, ultimately, *managers must do things* toward that end.

What Activities Do Managers Perform?

Managerial responsibilities provide the overarching framework and strategic direction for a manager, defining the purpose and objectives of their role. Activities, on the other hand, are the specific behaviors and tasks managers undertake to fulfill those responsibilities on a day-to-day basis. While responsibilities guide the manager's focus and priorities, activities are the practical manifestations of those responsibilities in the ongoing management of people, processes, and projects. Like I always say: you can't do anything without doing something.

> **You can't do anything without doing *something*.**

Consider this: although the baker understands the core principles of baking a delicious cake, has adapted their process to incorporate modern conveniences and available ingredients, understands the best practices of successful cake baking that have been passed down from all of the greats, and has all of the necessary ingredients, the baker still has to do stuff to deliver a delicious cake. Management principles provide the foundational concepts that guide managerial decision-making, responsibilities outline the overarching duties of a manager, and activities represent the specific, hands-on tasks that managers perform to fulfill their responsibilities in alignment with the principles.

So, what do managers *do*—the activities required of the position—on a daily basis? The specific activities that managers engage in as part of their role vary depending on the size and type of organization they work in, as well as their specific department or function. However, some common activities in which managers may engage are included in the table below.

To make for easier digestion of the material, I grouped the core activities by common theme where possible. These buckets provide a broad categorization based on common themes and functions, helping to highlight the interconnectedness of certain management activities and their alignment with specific aspects of organizational management.

ON MANAGEMENT

Strategic Management	Operational and Change Management	Leadership and People Management	Critical Thinking
• *Planning* • *Organizing* • *Budgeting* • *Risk Management*	• *Adaptability* • *Controlling* • *Staffing* • *Innovation* • *Project Management* • *Productivity*	• *Leading* • *Directing* • *Relationship Building* • *Emotional Intelligence* • *Communication* • *Delegation* • *Talent Management* • *Performance Management* • *Negotiation*	• *Decision Making* • *Problem-solving*

STRATEGIC MANAGEMENT

Planning

Managers are responsible for setting goals and objectives, creating and implementing plans, and allocating resources in a way that helps the company achieve its objectives.

Organizing

Managers must organize their department or team to ensure that all tasks are completed effectively and efficiently. They may assign tasks to employees, delegate responsibilities, and ensure that everyone is working together effectively.

Budgeting

Managers must prepare and manage budgets to ensure that the company's finances are under control. It allows managers to make informed decisions about budgeting, staffing, and resource allocation.

Risk Management

The ability to identify and manage potential risks to the organization. This skill is considered very effective as it allows managers to anticipate and respond to potential issues that may impact the organization.

OPERATIONAL AND CHANGE MANAGEMENT

Adaptability

The ability to adjust to changes in the marketplace and within the organization. This skill is considered very effective as it allows managers to anticipate and respond to changes in a timely and efficient manner.

Controlling

Managers must monitor performance metrics, financials, and other key indicators to ensure that the company is on track to achieve its goals. They must also be prepared to adjust their plans as necessary.

Staffing

Managers must hire, train, and supervise employees, and they must ensure that everyone is working effectively and efficiently. They must also evaluate employee performance and provide feedback and coaching as necessary.

Innovation

The ability to come up with new and creative ideas. This skill is considered very effective as it allows managers to develop new products, services, and strategies that will benefit the organization.

Project Management

The ability to plan, organize, and manage projects effectively. This skill is considered very effective as it allows managers to ensure that projects are completed on time and within budget.

Productivity

Managers must be able to ensure that priority activities that achieve KPIs are completed above all else. This ensures that managers and employees have adequate time to achieve job success and balance the work and life paradigms.

LEADERSHIP AND PEOPLE MANAGEMENT

Leading

Motivating and inspiring team members and providing guidance and direction to ensure that they are working towards the goals of the organization.

Relationship Building

Building and maintaining positive relationships with stakeholders, such as customers, vendors, and other teams within the organization.

Communication

Managers must communicate effectively with employees, other managers, and senior leaders. They must be able to present ideas and information clearly and persuasively, and they must be able to listen actively and respond appropriately.

Directing

Guiding, leading, and overseeing the execution of plans to achieve organizational goals. It involves providing clear instructions, motivation, and communication to ensure that employees or team members understand their roles and responsibilities.

Talent Management

Attracting, developing, and retaining skilled individuals to meet current and future organizational needs. The ability to identify and develop the skills and abilities of team members to ensure that individuals with the right skills and potential are available to fill critical roles.

Performance Management

The ability to evaluate the performance of team members and provide feedback and recognition. This skill is considered very effective as it allows managers to ensure that team members are meeting the organization's goals and standards.

Delegation

The ability to assign tasks to team members and delegate responsibility effectively. This skill is considered very effective as it allows managers to ensure that tasks are completed efficiently and effectively, while also developing the skills of team members.

Negotiation

The ability to negotiate effectively with stakeholders, suppliers, and other individuals. This skill is considered very effective as it allows managers to build and maintain relationships and ensure that the organization's goals are met.

Emotional Intelligence

The ability to understand and manage one's own emotions, as well as the emotions of others. This skill is considered very effective as it allows managers to build strong relationships and handle difficult situations in a calm and professional manner.

CRITICAL THINKING

Decision Making

Motivating and inspiring team members and providing guidance and direction to ensure that they are working towards the goals of the organization.

Problem Solving

Managers must be able to identify and resolve problems that arise in their department or team. They must also be able to make difficult decisions and implement effective solutions.

These are just a few of the many activities that managers engage in as part of their role. Ultimately, the specific activities that managers engage in will vary depending on the size and type of organization they work in, as well as their specific department or function.

Activity or Skill?

I can appreciate how, when reviewing each of these activities, one might ask, "Wait a minute. Isn't 'communication' a *skill?*" The answer is yes. There is, however, a clear distinction between, for instance, "communication" as a management activity and "communication" as a skill.

The distinction between a manager's activities and the corresponding skills boils down to *application* and *proficiency*. Managerial activities refer to the tangible tasks and responsibilities that a manager undertakes on a day-to-day basis to fulfill their role effectively. These encompass a spectrum of actions such as planning, organizing, directing, and controlling, each contributing to the overall success of the team or organization. These activities are observable, measurable, and represent the operational dimensions of managerial work.

On the other hand, managerial *skills* are the underlying competencies and proficiencies that enable a manager to perform these activities adeptly. Skills such as leadership, communication, problem-solving, and decision-making are paramount in executing managerial activities with finesse. For instance, effective communication skills are essential in conveying strategic objectives and fostering a positive work culture, while strong decision-making skills empower a manager to navigate complex situations and make sound choices. The skills encompass a blend of cognitive abilities, interpersonal acumen, and emotional intelligence that collectively define a manager's capability to handle the multifaceted challenges inherent in their role.

In essence, while managerial activities represent the practical execution of a manager's responsibilities, managerial skills underpin the competence and effectiveness with which these activities are carried out. The synergy between activities and skills is integral to managerial success, as proficiency in the latter enhances the execution and impact of the former.

> **More than half of all people with the job title of "manager" do not perform these activities collectively.**

At a minimum, these are the activities in which anyone holding the manager title should engage toward achieving desired outcomes and success in the job. What I find interesting is that, while nearly every new manager or those who have taken a management course have learned about the necessity of these management fundamentals, more than half of all managers do not perform all these activities, even when they are a part of their job description.

Our work with firms and their managers across company size, type, industry segment, and geography shows that more than half of all people with the job title of manager do not perform these activities collectively. When asked, they reveal that they know of the activities but simply do not perform them consistently or at all. We refer to this behavior as **Management by Ignorance.**

MANAGEMENT BY IGNORANCE

ON IGNORANCE

Let me start by saying that, in this context, I am not using the term "ignorance" in a derogatory manner. Instead, I am using it as the expression of an opportunity for managers to become more effective by growing in areas in which they may knowingly be deficient. A notable impediment to effective management lies in ignorance, which manifests as a dearth of knowledge, comprehension, or awareness in pivotal areas.

The ascent to the role of "Manager" often stands as a pivotal moment in one's career trajectory, yet far too frequently, individuals are propelled into this position without the essential skills, expertise, or experience necessary for effective leadership. This mismatch between title and preparedness creates a disconcerting reality where individuals find themselves stranded in a role that demands far more than they can deliver. This predicament not only hampers their personal growth but inflicts a ripple effect across their team and the organization at large. Their deficiencies cast a shadow over team morale, productivity dwindles, and the organizational fabric strains under the weight of mismanagement. It's a situation where everyone loses—a toxic cycle perpetuated by the mismatch between title and capability.

To be "ignorant" means to lack knowledge or awareness about a particular subject or a broader range of topics. It implies a lack of information, understanding, or familiarity with a particular subject matter, concept, or situation. Ignorance can be unintentional and may result from a lack of exposure, education, or experience. For instance, Jill, a newly promoted manager, does not know how to navigate and manage a profit & loss statement (P&L). Does that mean that Jill is a bad manager? No. Ineffective? Maybe. But bad? Not necessarily.

It could mean that Jill has yet to master that critical managerial function, even though she knows that doing so is a part of her job. This implies an opportunity for Jill to become a better manager by acquiring P&L knowledge and applying it toward the achievement of Key Performance Indicators (KPIs). Or, more damning, it could mean that she believes she is managing just fine and doesn't see the importance or urgency of acquiring P&L knowledge and skill. In this case, Jill is **managing by ignorance**: continuing to perform her job as a manager, knowing that managing a P&L is valuable in her role, but intentionally choosing not to make the effort to acquire the skills necessary to improve that part of her managerial repertoire.

The phenomenon of intentionally choosing to remain ignorant about something one knows is incorrect can be attributed to several psychological factors. *Cognitive Dissonance*, for instance, involves psychological discomfort that arises when a person holds two conflicting beliefs or attitudes. In order to alleviate this discomfort, individuals might opt to ignore or downplay evidence that contradicts their existing beliefs. Another contributing factor is *Confirmation Bias*, which manifests as the tendency to seek out, interpret, and remember information in a way that affirms one's preexisting beliefs or values. This can lead people to actively avoid information that challenges their existing views.

Other factors could also be at play, causing Jill to rationalize that managing a P&L is not an impediment to her receiving a good performance review rating. *Motivated Reasoning*, for instance, is a cognitive process where individuals tend to selectively process information in a manner that supports their preexisting views or goals. In doing so, they may engage in biased evaluation of evidence, favoring information that aligns with their established beliefs: "I get great performance evals from my boss, so what I am doing must be the best way to do my job."

Additionally, *self-esteem protection* plays a significant role, as admitting one's own wrongness or ignorance about something can be psychologically threatening, particularly if the belief is closely linked to one's identity or sense of self-worth. In some cases, ignorance serves as a defense mechanism to safeguard one's self-esteem. Other reasons could be *fear of change* which also contributes to this phenomenon, and *overconfidence bias* could come into play, where Jill may possess an inflated sense of her own knowledge and abilities, contributing to the psychological phenomenon of **intentional ignorance**, leading to *management by ignorance*.

> NOTE: With professional office-based workers, it is often the case that there is no correlation between performing all the responsibilities of one's job and their job performance rating. It is quite common for professionals to skate by, do the least amount of work possible, and still receive the highest job rating. The primary reason is most performance plans are poorly developed with no relationship between objective work proficiency and performance ratings. Because of this, such performance reviews have little to do with efficacy, rendering them mostly popularity contests or *based on other subjective criteria.*

It's important to note that ignorance is not necessarily a negative trait on its own. It simply signifies **a state of not knowing**. However, when ignorance leads to uninformed opinions or decisions, especially in situations where knowledge is crucial, it can become problematic. So, how does Jill begin to overcome management by ignorance? She must acknowledge her P&L ignorance or knowledge-shortcoming, consider it to be unacceptable—regardless of her performance review rating—and take steps to learn and gain knowledge in areas where it's lacking. Acknowledgment is the first step towards personal & professional growth and a more informed perspective as a manager or leader.

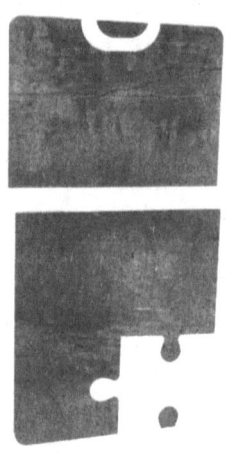

PART TWO
TRANSITION

CHAPTER THREE
FROM COMPETENT TO EXCEPTIONAL

As we delve into the heart of our managerial exploration, this chapter marks a pivotal shift in our learning journey. Thus far, our focus has been on laying the foundational principles of effective management—establishing the bedrock upon which successful leadership is built. We've navigated through the intricacies of planning, organizing, directing, controlling, and other managerial responsibilities, unraveling the blocks that build the structure of competent management. Now, it's time to set our sights higher, to transcend the status of adequacy and embark on a quest toward managerial excellence.

Competent management is characterized by proficiency in the fundamental skills and practices required for effective leadership. A competent manager can navigate routine tasks, uphold organizational standards, and ensure the team's day-to-day operations run smoothly. However, the essence of this chapter lies in the exploration of what lies beyond competence—the realm of exceptional management.

Exceptional management transcends the ordinary. It's about achieving results that go above and beyond expectations, fostering an environment of innovation, and inspiring a team to reach new heights. Exceptional managers are visionary leaders who not only meet but exceed organizational goals, leaving an indelible mark on their teams and the broader internal and external landscapes of their professional domain.

Consider this scenario.

Imagine management as a journey through a vast landscape, where the competent manager navigates well-trodden paths, ensuring a steady and reliable progression. Competent management is akin to driving a well-maintained car on a familiar road—a journey marked by efficiency, predictability, and a sense of security. The competent manager skillfully maneuvers through the landscape, meeting the expected milestones with precision.

Now, envision the transformation from competent to exceptional management as a shift from driving on established roads to soaring through uncharted skies. The exceptional manager doesn't settle for the comfort of familiar terrain but takes flight into the expansive possibilities of the open sky. It's like exchanging the well-driven car for a state-of-the-art aircraft—a vehicle designed not just for the journey but for the exploration of new heights and horizons.

In this metaphor, the competent manager operates within the boundaries of known roads, ensuring a smooth and reliable journey. On the other hand, the exceptional manager trades the road for the limitless sky, embracing challenges, navigating turbulence, and reaching destinations that were once beyond the horizon. The exceptional manager is not confined by the constraints of the road but rather aspires to soar to new altitudes, embracing the dynamic and ever-changing nature of the managerial landscape.

Moving from competent to exceptional is not a mere leap; it's a deliberate and transformative journey. It involves honing specific skills, adopting innovative approaches, and cultivating a mindset that thrives on strategy and continuous improvement. In the upcoming pages, we will dissect the practical elements that constitute this transformative process. From leveraging strategic intelligence to mastering the art of the action feedback cycle, we will explore the actionable steps that elevate *any* manager's proficiency from competent to exceptional.

A Practical Approach

To achieve the transformation, I will focus on a handful of practical management practices that most dramatically move a manager's effectiveness from sufficient to excellent—taking them from competent to exceptional. The practices I have specifically curated for this purpose are proven not only to improve a manager's effectiveness but to do so in the shortest amount of time with the greatest degree of measurable impact.

My colleagues and I have worked with managers and leaders ranging from those with no experience to those with vast experience, from SMBs to global enterprises, and in industries ranging from slow-moving to fast-paced, dynamic sectors. We have conducted our work on various continents. Through these experiences, we have identified five management practices that, if executed properly, will elevate a manager's proficiency in a short order. These include:

1. **Strategic Planning & Execution**
2. **Manager Proficiency Assessment**
3. **Emotional Safety**
4. **Performance Planning**
5. **Productivity**

MANAGEMENT PRACTICES
FOR EXCELLENCE

1. STRATEGIC PLANNING AND EXECUTION

Strategy: The Cornerstone OF Organizational Effectiveness

In the realm of organizational management, strategy stands as the cornerstone upon which all activities, decisions, and innovations are built. From the hallowed halls of leading business schools to the profound insights of revered management thinkers, the significance of a well-crafted strategy reverberates as the driver that charts the course for organizational success.

Strategy plays a critical role in achieving sustainable competitive advantage and long-term prosperity. Aspiring managers are taught to view strategy not merely as a document but as a *dynamic process* that aligns an organization's strengths with external opportunities while mitigating potential threats. Unfortunately, most managers do not.

The idea that a robust strategy is not only a roadmap for success but a core principle that steers the organization through ever-changing business landscapes should be ingrained into the psyche of management practitioners just as, for example, the main cable of a bridge is considered an essential structural requirement for bridge-building civil engineers.

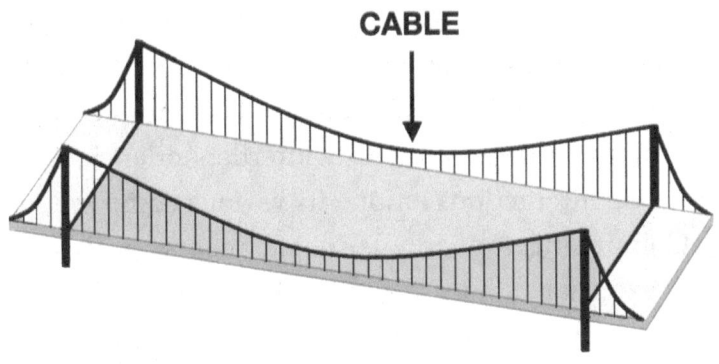

Like an organization, business unit, department, or team, a bridge is an example of something where the removal of one key foundational element (e.g., a well-reasoned strategy for an organization) can lead to failure, as in a suspension bridge. In the design of a suspension bridge, several crucial components work in tandem to ensure structural integrity and support the bridge's weight. One of the key foundational elements is the *main cables*.

If you remove or compromise one of the main cables of a suspension bridge, the entire structure is at risk of catastrophic failure. The main cables bear the majority of the load and provide essential support to the bridge deck. Any damage or removal of these cables disrupts the delicate balance of forces, jeopardizing the stability of the entire bridge. Without the strength and tension provided by the main cables, the bridge is unable to distribute the loads effectively, leading to a collapse. In this sense, a well-reasoned strategy is like a bridge's main cable.

This example illustrates the importance of recognizing and preserving key foundational elements in complex systems; **an organization is a complex system** characterized by intricate interdependencies and dynamic interactions among its various components.

Comprising individuals, departments, processes, and external factors, an organization's complexity arises from the multifaceted relationships that influence its functioning. The organizational structure, culture, and communication networks form intricate patterns, akin to a web—or a bridge—where changes in one area can reverberate throughout the system. Understanding and managing this complexity necessitate a holistic perspective, recognizing that the organization is not merely a sum of its parts but an interconnected and dynamic system that requires **strategic and adaptive approaches for sustained success.**

In various contexts, whether in engineering, organizational management, or other fields, the removal or compromise of a critical component, like an effective strategy, can have far-reaching consequences, highlighting the interconnected nature of foundational elements within a system.

Management thinkers, including luminaries like Peter Drucker and Michael Porter, have consistently underscored the centrality of strategy in organizational effectiveness. A well-crafted strategy serves as a unifying force within an organization, aligning diverse functions and activities toward common objectives. It provides a framework for decision-making, ensuring that every action contributes to the overarching goals of the organization. In essence, strategy serves as the north star, guiding leaders and employees alike in their daily pursuits.

> **If you get the strategy piece wrong, then everything else falls apart.**

The significance of a strategy as the foundation for everything in an organization cannot be overstated. It is the culmination of insights and the wisdom of management thinkers, educators, and experienced practitioners alike. A well-defined strategy empowers organizations to set clear objectives, navigate complexities, and remain agile in the face of change. As a guiding force, strategy propels organizations toward excellence, ensuring that every endeavor contributes to the overarching vision and mission. Therefore, it is not only important to manage by strategy (including management by objectives, popularized by Peter Drucker in his 1954 book "The Practice of Management," and management by initiatives, as I developed in my book "MBI: Management By Initiatives"), but it is equally important to get the strategy piece right! If you get it wrong, then everything else falls apart.

Understanding Strategy and Alignment

A **strategy** is a plan for achieving desired outcomes. It is the process that translates purpose into action. **Strategic planning** is the process organizations follow to set the direction for the organization, allocate its resources to support that direction, define how it's going to get there, and determine how it will know whether it got there within the desired timeframe. Put differently, strategic planning is the process of creating a strategy. A strategic plan is an explicitly stated documentation of a strategy. In that sense, a strategy and a strategic plan are synonymous.

A strategy is a vehicle for aligning all of an organization's plans toward the fulfillment of a unified, common goal, driving alignment between all of an organization's business units and functional areas, and eliminating inconsistencies and wastes of effort & resources.

In our 2015 study, which focused on managers with people responsibilities (commonly referred to as *supervisors*) in *Fortune* 500 firms and those with 1,000 or more employees, we found that a staggering 86% of the managers in the study group lacked proficiency or even fundamental competence in strategic planning and thinking. This skill—combined with leadership—is arguably the most crucial for effective management since it is foundational. Put differently, if a manager is not proficient at strategic planning, they will struggle to achieve sustainable success.

Elements of a Strategy: Goals, Objectives, and Action Plans

A strategy fundamentally expresses an organization's desired future state and the as-of-today requirements to get there. An organization will define a long-term vision of what it wants to be or become in some future, multi-year timeframe. To fulfill this vision, the organization must develop a plan for how it will get there, a plan consisting of shorter-term targets and milestones referred to as **goals** and **objectives**, and a supporting **action plan** to achieve said goals and objectives.

Goals

A goal is a broad, often-qualitative intended outcome of an initiative or an activity in which the company is engaged that indicates success or improvement in organizational performance or a reinforcement of the organization's values; they are the outcomes an organization must achieve if it is to effectively work toward its mission and achieve its vision. Goals take the form of "To [Action Verb] [Noun]" and are not always achievable in the desired short-to-medium-term timeframe. For example, a market development goal could be "To become the #2 software provider in the Northeast Region of United States (in dollar sales)."

Objectives

An objective is a Key Performance Indicator and the measurable (usually quantitative) manifestation of the goal which it supports. In other words, the objective defines in measurable/quantitative (and time-specific) terms how the company will know that it has accomplished the goal which the objective supports. For example, if a goal is "To become the #2 software provider in the Northeast Region of the United States (in dollar sales)" and, last year, the #2 software provider sold $X in software, then the objective supporting the goal would be defined in such a way that, if the objective is achieved, the company would know it had accomplished its goal. For example, a supporting objective could be: "Achieve $X + $1 in software sales by December 31st."

Initiatives

Once the goal(s) and objectives are defined, specific "initiatives" must be articulated to support the objectives. An initiative is a project or other undertaking that defines what must be done to achieve the objective it supports. So, if the objective is to "Achieve $X + $1 in software sales by December 31st," the associated initiative(s) must define the project(s) that will lead to $X + $1 million in sales by December 31st.

Tasks and Action Items

Once the Initiatives are defined, a set of tasks or action items must be developed which define the specific activities that must be executed to realize the initiative it supports. Each task or action item must define the person who is accountable for task completion and has ultimate ownership for it, and the person who is responsible for executing the task (i.e., does the work) if that person is different from the person who is accountable for task completion. Furthermore, the resources (human resources, money, third party extensions, and tools, etc.) that will be needed to complete a task must be identified.

Action Plan

The action plan makes the strategy "real" and tangible for an organization's personnel. It translates an organization's vision and mission into tangible objectives, measures, and executable actions. Many people mistakenly believe that a strategy's action plan is the collective set of tasks to be performed to realize the associated initiative; that is incorrect. **The action plan portion of a strategy includes all elements that make the goal real**, including the quantitative/measurable objectives, the related initiatives, and the associated tasks. This relationship is illustrated in the diagram below.

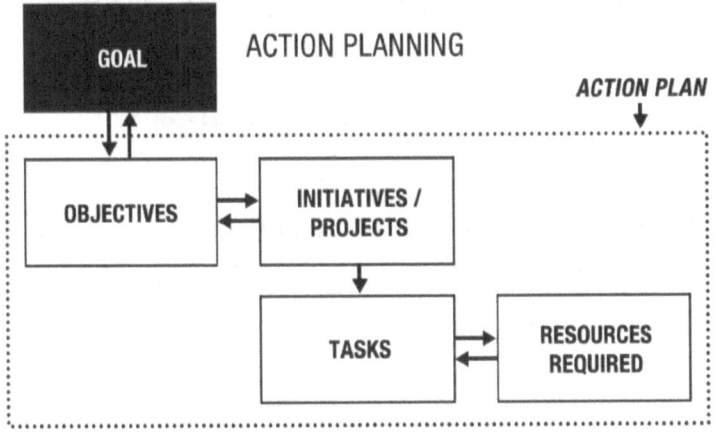

Note: Goals Inform Objectives

In a strategic planning context, goals and objectives are related but serve different purposes. Goals are broad, overarching statements that express the overall aims or desired outcomes of an organization. Objectives, on the other hand, are more specific, measurable, and time-bound targets that contribute to the achievement of goals. The phrase "goals inform objectives" suggests that the establishment of objectives should be guided by the overarching goals of the organization. In other words, the goals set by an organization provide the direction and context for defining specific objectives. **Objectives are then designed to support and contribute to the accomplishment of these broader goals**. This relationship ensures alignment and coherence in the strategic planning process, as objectives are essentially the actionable steps taken to reach the more general aspirations outlined in the goals.

ON MANAGEMENT

Causality: Cause and Effect Relationship

"A strategy is a hypothesis about cause and effect."

Richard Rumelt, *renowned strategy scholar and professor of business and society at the University of California, Los Angeles (UCLA)*

Effective plans or strategies must contain relationships that follow **cause-and-effect logic**, eliminating coincidence as much as possible. Cause-and-effect supposes that if you do "A," then "B" will happen as a direct result of having done "A." If you do not do "A," however, then "B" will not happen. The "if-then" nature of strategy holds that once we undertake an action, we expect that the outcome of the action (an outcome we predicted would occur before we took the action) actually occurs. In a well-developed plan, this cause-and-effect relationship will exist between goals and objectives; objectives and initiatives; and initiatives and tasks.

1. If I perform an action item, it will lead to the completion of an initiative or project.
2. If I complete the initiatives, it will lead to the achievement of their associated objective.
3. If I achieve the objectives, I will have accomplished their associated goal(s).

The cause-and-effect relationships between the elements of a strategy are depicted in the diagram below.

Whereas goals, objectives, and initiatives have informative strengths, tasks influence the resources required to achieve them. Informative strength implies that goals, objectives, and initiatives prescribe and are directly aligned with the supporting elements of a strategy; they serve as a primary source of guidance. To "influence" suggests a broader impact or shaping effect that tasks have on resource requirements. This phrase indicates that while tasks play a role in shaping resources supplied, there may be additional factors or considerations that also contribute to the provisioning of specific resources. The influence may be indirect or may involve a more dynamic and interactive relationship between task needs and resources provided. In essence, both expressions highlight the idea that there is a relationship between all of the elements in the context of strategic planning.

The Importance of Key Performance Indicators in a Strategic Plan: Execution

Key Performance Indicators (KPIs) serve as the compass in navigating the strategic plan. They are not just metrics; **they are the pulse of strategic execution.** In a well-crafted strategic plan, KPIs illuminate progress, providing invaluable insights into whether the organization is on course to achieve its intended objectives. To paraphrase Scottish Philosopher Thomas Carlyle, without KPIs, strategy becomes a ship without a rudder, drifting in the vast sea of uncertainties. They are the cornerstone of strategic success, offering a quantifiable measure of alignment, progress, and ultimately, the realization of strategic goals. As you move forward through this book, keep in mind that *KPIs are the pulse of strategic execution.* And execution, in my experience, is the most significant problem organizations struggle with when trying to implement a strategy.

A common mistake often highlighted in the field of strategic planning is the failure to effectively implement the strategic plan. Many business schools, researchers, and strategic planning authorities emphasize that crafting a well-thought-out strategy is just one part of the process, and **the real challenge lies in the execution**. The biggest mistake organizations make is often seen as not translating their strategic plans into actionable steps or failing to align the implementation with the overall goals. This could include insufficient communication of the strategy throughout the organization, a lack of engagement from key stakeholders, inadequate resource allocation, or an inability to adapt to changing circumstances. Ultimately, however, the success of a strategic plan is contingent on its effective execution, and organizations that neglect or mismanage the implementation phase may struggle to realize the intended benefits of their strategic initiatives.

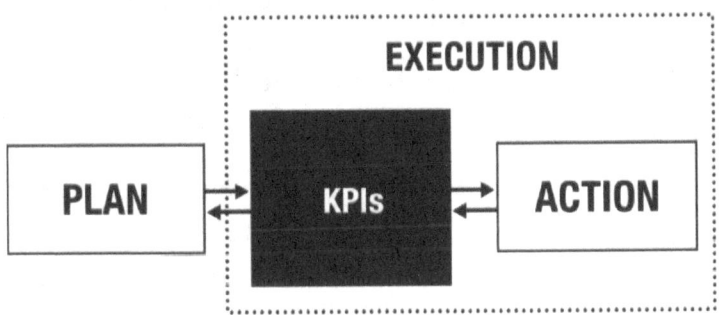

Key Performance Indicators are often referred to by various terms, reflecting their role in assessing and measuring performance in different contexts. They often include terms like objectives, various metrics,

Key Success or Results Indicators, value drivers, Critical Success Factors, Benchmark Indicators, and others. Regardless of which term is used, the concept remains consistent: to enable execution, a strategy must include specific, measurable indicators of progress toward the goals and success.

Crafting Key Performance Indicators: Three Questions

Objectives are the most common form of KPI managers use in developing strategies or crafting employees' performance plan targets. To determine whether KPIs or objectives are well-defined and in the organization's best interest, the manager must be able to honestly answer the following three questions:

1. **How will you know, unequivocally**, that this KPI/objective has been successfully achieved?
2. **For each objective, can you answer the question:** "How much and by when?" For example, if an objective is "to increase sales in Boston," you must be able to articulate what represents an increase in sales (e.g., new customers, revenue growth, etc.), how much sales must specifically be increased to or increased by to meet a necessary target, and by when does the sales increase amount need to be achieved.

3. During the performance review and appraisal meeting between you and your team members, **will you both completely agree about their success at achieving this objective** and the degree to which it has been achieved? Using the previous example of increasing sales in Boston, will there be any ambiguity, misunderstanding, uncertainty, lack of clarity, disagreement, or debate about the specific sales increase form and target amount and the deadline date for achieving the target amount?

| How will you know that this KPI has been successfully achieved? | For each objective, can you answer the question: "How much and by when?" | Will you completely agree about their success at achieving this objective |

Although SMART criteria are commonly associated with Peter Drucker's management by objectives concept, the idea that goals and objectives/KPIs should be written in a S.M.A.R.T. way was proposed by a consultant and former director of corporate planning for Washington Water Power Company named George T. Doran. In the November 1981 issue of *Management Review (AMA Forum)*, a paper by Doran called *There's a S.M.A.R.T. way to write management's goals and objectives* discussed the importance of objectives and the difficulty of setting them. He wrote that, ideally speaking, each corporate, department, and section objective should be:

- *Specific*: target a specific area for improvement.
- *Measurable*: quantify or at least suggest an indicator of progress.
- *Assignable*: specify who will do it.
- *Realistic*: state which results can realistically be achieved, given available resources.
- *Time-related*: specify when the result(s) can be achieved.

Yes, I know; S.M.A.R.T objectives are management 101. However, I believe their inclusion is necessary since, although all managers agree that objectives should be "smart," very few managers apply the principle consistently—if at all—when crafting objectives/KPIs for their business units, departments, teams, or even employees' performance plans.

> **Even if you cannot quantify every target outcome, it is critical that both you—the manager—and your direct reports each agree on what will unambiguously determine the successful achievement of each non-quantifiable performance indicator.**

It is worth noting that not all objectives must be quantified at all levels of management. In certain situations, it is not realistic to quantify everything, particularly in staff middle-management positions. However, even if you cannot quantify every target outcome, it is critical that both you—the manager—and your direct reports each agree on what will unambiguously determine the successful achievement of each non-quantifiable performance indicator. For example, if you craft a KPI to **"improve employee morale,"** you must be prepared to answer the questions below, and you and your direct report must both agree on the satisfaction criteria for that KPI:

1. What does employee morale mean?

2. What is the current benchmark state of employee morale?

3. How will we know that employee morale has changed? Increased?

4. What criteria will we use to gauge a change in morale?

5. What will a satisfactory employee morale increase actually look like, and if, at the end of the performance measurement period, we observe this condition, will we both agree that the KPI has successfully been achieved?

KPI FORMAT TIPS

When crafting KPIs or objectives, consider using the following format as a guide to increase the chances that they are created effectively.

To [ACTION VERB] [NOUN] by/to [VALUE] by [DEADLINE]

Crafting objectives using strong and specific action verbs is crucial for clarity and precision. These verbs help define the measurable actions or outcomes you aim to achieve. As an example, here are some effective action verbs commonly used in crafting measurable objectives:

Increase:

- Increase revenue by 15%.
- Increase customer satisfaction scores to 90%.

Decrease:

- Decrease production errors by 20%.
- Decrease response time to customer inquiries by 30%.

Improve:

- Improve employee productivity by 25%.
- Improve on-time delivery rates to 95%.

Enhance:

- Enhance product quality through process improvements.
- Enhance brand visibility in the target market.

Expand:
- Expand market share by 10%.
- Expand the customer base by entering new markets.

Optimize:
- Optimize supply chain efficiency.
- Optimize website conversion rates.

Achieve:
- Achieve a customer retention rate of 90%.
- Achieve a 98% completion rate for project tasks.

Attain:
- Attain a safety incident rate of zero.
- Attain 100% compliance with industry standards.

Implement:
- Implement a new employee training program.
- Implement a system for real-time performance tracking.

Launch:
- Launch a new product line by Q3.
- Launch a marketing campaign targeting a new demographic.

Reduce:
- Reduce energy consumption by 15%.
- Reduce inventory holding costs by 20%.

Maximize:

- Maximize customer lifetime value.
- Maximize efficiency in production processes.

Minimize:

- Minimize project delays.
- Minimize waste in manufacturing processes.

Establish:

- Establish a strong online presence.
- Establish a cross-functional collaboration initiative.

Streamline:

- Streamline communication processes.
- Streamline project management workflows.

Others include improve, gain, eliminate, grow, phase out, and more.

NOTE: In cases where KPIs are not measurable, ensure to reach an agreement with employees on how you will unequivocally determine whether a KPI has been successfully achieved.

FROM COMPETENT TO EXCEPTIONAL

THREE PILLARS OF MANAGERIAL JOB SUCCESS

Answer the following two questions:

1. What is the number one job responsibility of a manager?

2. What is the second most important responsibility of a manager?

The answers to these questions will provide invaluable insight into what separates good managers from great managers, competent managers from exceptional managers. Some argue that, depending on the market in which the manager's firm operates, the responsibilities assigned to the manager per their job description and performance plan, the manager's level in the organizational hierarchy (C-level managers may have a different focus than a first-line manager), and the needs of the business, the manager's primary and secondary responsibilities can vary.

Peter Drucker, often regarded as the father of modern management, emphasized various aspects of managerial responsibilities throughout his extensive body of work. One of the key principles associated with Drucker's perspective is his emphasis on the ultimate purpose of a business and, consequently, the primary responsibility of a manager. According to Drucker, the primary responsibility of a manager in a firm is to create and maintain a customer. Drucker argued that without customers, a business has no reason to exist, and it is through the creation and retention of customers that a business achieves success and sustainability.

Michael Porter, a renowned economist and professor at Harvard Business School, is known for his contributions to strategic management and competitive advantage. While Porter hasn't explicitly outlined a single, overarching responsibility for managers, his work suggests several key areas of focus that are critical for managerial success. Porter emphasizes the importance of strategy and competitive positioning in his work.

Robert S. Kaplan and David P. Norton, known for their work on the Balanced Scorecard, emphasize a broader set of managerial responsibilities that go beyond traditional financial metrics. According to Kaplan and Norton, the primary responsibility of a manager involves managing and aligning the organization's strategy and performance.

Tom Peters, a management guru and co-author of the influential book "In Search of Excellence," emphasizes several principles related to effective management. While he doesn't prescribe a single, specific responsibility as the number one for all managers, Peters often underscores the importance of people-centric leadership and fostering a culture of innovation and excellence.

While I acknowledge that these are all valid perspectives, my position closely aligns with that of Tom Peters, a manager whose work and thought leadership I have admired since my early days as a manager and consultant. Peters emphasizes the critical role of managers as leaders and people developers, what he referred to as a **people-centric nature of effective management**. Managers, he believes, should focus on empowering their teams, providing support, and creating an environment where individuals can excel.

His new concept "Extreme Humanism," as he calls it, encourages businesses to put their people first.

Peters also values a results-oriented approach to management, where managers should be focused on achieving tangible outcomes and driving the organization toward its goals. These areas of emphasis are consistent with what I have found to be, from a practical standpoint, the two things that managers do that lead to the most significant contribution to job success: employee success and the manager's individual success—which is not possible without the former.

So, what are the answers to the two questions? Based on the practical, real-world performance of managers we have assessed, evaluated, studied, engaged, trained, and coached, we propose that the answers are as follows:

1. What is the number one job responsibility of a manager?

The number one job responsibility of a manager is *to ensure the success of their direct report employees.* This is consistent with the people-centric nature of effective management and Tom Peters' concept of Extreme Humanism—putting people first.

FROM COMPETENT TO EXCEPTIONAL

If an organization's goals and objectives are aligned throughout the organization, cascaded through every level of employees and their jobs, then a manager cannot achieve job success (determined by achieving KPIs) unless each of their employees achieves their individual job success. A manager's obligations are carried out by their employees.

For example, if a manager is charged with generating and delivering the sale of 100 pizzas by the end of the week, the manager will cascade this objective equitably to each of their employees. As each employee successfully sells their 20 pizzas (their individual, cascaded, aligned KPI), the pizza sales will collectively roll up to the manager, who, because of the employees' individual success, is able to achieve job success by delivering the sale of 100 pizzas, the manager's KPI.

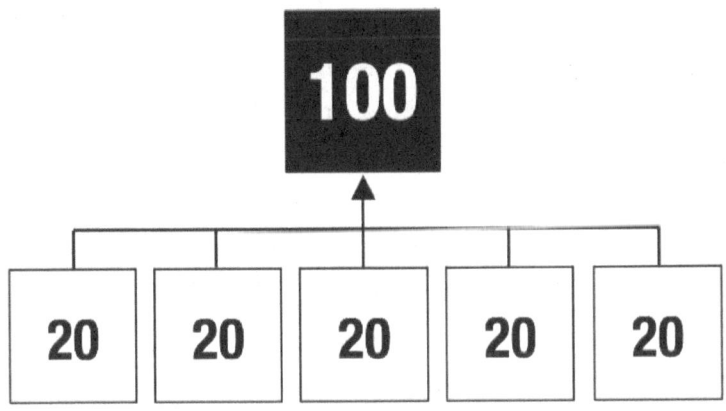

Conversely, the employees cannot achieve their individual job success without the manager's support and enablement; this is the second most important responsibility of a manager.

2. What is the second most important responsibility of a manager?

The manager's individual job success is contingent upon the collective success of their employees. Therefore, it is in the manager's best interest to ensure that they are doing everything they can to help the employees succeed. If the manager is to be successful, they must *enable the success of their employees.*

Success enablement in the manager-employee relationship refers to the proactive efforts and strategies employed by a manager to empower and support their employees in achieving individual and collective success. It is more than the obvious aspect of enablement, namely, making sure employees have the tools (e.g., software platforms) to do their jobs effectively. It involves creating an environment where employees can thrive, develop their skills, and contribute meaningfully to the organization's goals. Success enablement goes beyond traditional management practices by emphasizing collaboration, growth, and fostering a sense of purpose.

One aspect of success enablement is providing clear expectations and aligning individual goals with organizational objectives. Managers must communicate the company's mission, vision, and strategic priorities, *ensuring that employees understand how their work contributes to the overall success of the organization.* This clarity helps employees see the bigger picture, fostering a sense of purpose and motivation.

Additionally, success enablement involves offering resources and opportunities for professional development. Managers should actively support their employees' growth by providing training programs, mentorship, and access to relevant resources. For example, a manager could identify a team member's interest in a particular skill set and sponsor them to attend a relevant training workshop or assign them to a project where they can apply and enhance those skills. By investing in employees' development, managers not only contribute to individual success but also strengthen the team's overall capabilities, driving organizational success.

> **The manager and the worker share responsibility for each other's success. Therefore, it should be mandatory that the manager is fully vested and engaged in the worker's performance and job success.** –*From* "Doing Your Job: Successfully"

The manager and the worker share responsibility for each other's success. Therefore, it should be mandatory that the manager is fully vested and engaged in the worker's performance and job success.

In addition to ensuring and enabling employees' job success, there is a third pillar of managerial job success: achieving their own job success.

A manager's individual job success is intricately tied to the performance of their direct reports, yet it often involves additional criteria or Key Performance Indicators (KPIs) that go beyond the collective KPIs of the manager's team. While the success of the team is paramount for a manager, organizations recognize that managerial roles encompass broader responsibilities that contribute to the overall health and strategic direction of the business. These additional criteria typically reflect the manager's ability to align the team's efforts with organizational goals, foster innovation, and effectively communicate and execute strategic initiatives.

For instance, consider a sales manager overseeing a team responsible for regional revenue targets. While the team's KPIs focus on achieving sales quotas and customer satisfaction metrics, the manager's individual success may be evaluated based on factors such as the successful implementation of a new sales strategy, the development of high-performing team members, or the establishment of key partnerships that enhance the overall market presence. In this scenario, the manager's KPIs extend beyond the direct sales figures of the team and encompass strategic leadership, talent development, and contributions to the organization's growth and market positioning.

This approach acknowledges that effective managerial performance involves not only achieving immediate operational goals but also aligning team efforts with broader organizational objectives. By incorporating these additional criteria into a manager's evaluation, organizations aim to ensure that managerial roles are not solely focused on short-term outcomes but contribute to the long-term success and sustainability of the business.

ON MANAGEMENT

The Manager's Impact on Employee Success

The Corporate Leadership Council (CLC), in its extensive study titled *Driving Employee Performance and Retention Through Engagement*, has identified 160 broadly applied levers that contribute to overall workforce engagement. The more levers an organization lacks proficiency in, the lower the potential for its employees to be fully engaged at work. Consider the "Qualities of the Direct Manager" lever, which encompasses attributes defined by the CLC, such as:

- Commitment to Diversity;
- Demonstrates Honesty and Integrity;
- Adapts to Changing Circumstances;
- Clearly Articulates Organizational Goals;
- Possesses Job Skills; and
- Sets Realistic Performance Expectations.

This set of manager-controlled levers directly influences a worker's motivation, effort, performance, commitment, and propensity to remain with the organization. There's an old saying that "People don't quit a job, they quit a boss." While this may not always be the sole reason for voluntary job departures, individuals are indeed more likely to quit if they have a problematic boss. A 2015 Gallup study discovered that approximately 50% of the 7,200 surveyed adults had left a job "to get away from their manager." Interestingly, over half of the respondents gave the "highest agreement rating" to the statement, "I feel I can approach my manager with any type of question." These engaged workers, as per *The Wall Street Journal*, imply that manager openness may be linked to engagement and worker productivity.

A meaningful gauge of the strength of the employee-manager relationship is **the comfort level an employee experiences when approaching their manager with any type of question**, a comfort influenced by the aforementioned list of manager qualities and the manager's ability to create a safe environment.

> **A 2015 Gallup study discovered that approximately 50% of the 7,200 surveyed adults had left a job "to get away from their manager."**

Why Managers Have Such an Impact on Employee Success, Failure, and Intent to Stay

Recent research consistently underscores the critical role of managers in influencing the success or failure of employees. The impact of managers extends beyond day-to-day operations, with deep implications for employee engagement, job satisfaction, and overall performance. One key factor is the manager's direct influence on the work environment, team dynamics, and organizational culture.

Effective managers play a pivotal role in creating a positive work culture that fosters collaboration, innovation, and employee well-being. Their leadership style, communication skills, and ability to provide clear expectations significantly contribute to shaping the workplace atmosphere. **Research indicates that employees who perceive their managers as supportive, transparent, and empowering are more likely to thrive and contribute positively to the organization.**

Managers are also instrumental in facilitating career development and growth opportunities for their team members. Research highlights the impact of mentorship, coaching, and personalized feedback provided by managers on employees' professional advancement. Managers who actively invest in the development of their team contribute to higher levels of job satisfaction, increased motivation, and a greater sense of purpose among employees.

Moreover, recent studies emphasize the direct correlation between managerial effectiveness and employee retention. A manager's ability to create a positive work experience, address challenges, and recognize individual contributions significantly influences employees' decisions to stay with an organization.

In essence, the latest research emphasizes that managers serve as linchpins in shaping organizational success **by influencing the employee experience**, fostering a positive work culture, and driving individual and collective performance. Their impact extends far beyond task management, encompassing the broader aspects of leadership, mentorship, and creating an environment conducive to employee growth and success.

The anatomy of job success, depicted below, illustrates just how many levers of employee job success are controlled and influenced by the manager.

THE ANATOMY OF JOB SUCCESS
Job fit
Internal support and training
Worker engagement
Alignment between org. goals and worker performance plan
SMART KPIs
Impact on job success

10 Common Managerial Mistakes

All managers make mistakes, regardless of their number of years of experience. The most common managerial mistakes involving employees include:

1. *Lack of communication*: Not effectively communicating goals, expectations, and feedback to team members, which can lead to confusion, low morale, and poor performance.

2. *Micromanaging*: Being overly involved in the day-to-day work of team members, which can stifle creativity and innovation, and lead to demotivation.

3. *Lack of delegation:* Not delegating tasks and responsibilities to team members, which can lead to burnout and resentment.

4. *Failing to provide clear expectations*: Not providing clear expectations for performance and goals, which can lead to confusion and poor performance.

5. *Not setting realistic goals*: Setting unrealistic goals that cannot be achieved, which can lead to disappointment and demotivation.

6. *Neglecting to give feedback*: Not providing regular feedback to team members, which can lead to misunderstandings, poor performance, and low morale.

7. *Failing to recognize and reward good performance*: Not recognizing and rewarding good performance, which can lead to demotivation and a lack of engagement.

8. *Not providing opportunities for professional development*: Not providing opportunities for team members to develop their skills and advance their careers, which can lead to a lack of engagement and high turnover.

9. *Not being adaptable*: Not being adaptable and open to change, which can lead to resistance to new ideas and a lack of innovation.

10. *Not handling conflicts well:* Not handling conflicts well, which can lead to a hostile work environment and low morale.

A manager's mistakes can have profound repercussions on their employees and the overall dynamics within a team or organization. The manager serves as a leader whose plans employees follow. And their decisions, whether strategic or operational, directly influence the work environment. Errors in judgment, lack of clear communication, or inconsistent leadership can lead to confusion, demotivation, and a decline in employee morale. Employees often look to their managers for direction, support, and a sense of stability. When a manager makes mistakes, it can erode trust and confidence in their leadership. This can result in decreased job satisfaction, diminished productivity, and an increased likelihood of turnover.

Moreover, a manager's mistakes may set a negative precedent for problem-solving and decision-making within the team, potentially hindering collaboration and hindering overall success. It underscores the importance of managers acknowledging and learning from their mistakes to foster a positive work environment and maintain a high level of employee engagement.

The Impact of Poor Management Practices

The paper titled *The Effects of Bad Management on Employee Job Satisfaction and Turnover Intentions* by Lau and Wood (2006) investigates the impact of poor management practices on employee job satisfaction and their intentions to leave the organization. The study acknowledges the crucial role that effective management plays in shaping the work environment and employee experiences. The authors explore how specific managerial behaviors and practices contribute to employees' job satisfaction and influence their likelihood of considering leaving their current positions.

The research delves into the **dimensions of bad management**, including factors such as lack of communication, inadequate recognition, and unfair treatment. The findings shed light on the intricate relationship between management practices and employee outcomes. Poor management is identified as a significant predictor of reduced job satisfaction among employees. Additionally, the research highlights the correlation between unsatisfactory management and higher turnover intentions, indicating that employees subjected to unfavorable management conditions are more likely to contemplate leaving their jobs.

These findings align with those of Robbins, Judge, & Sanghi, whose 2009 paper on *The Impact of Poor Management on Employee Job Performance and Satisfaction* investigated the relationship between poor management practices and employee job performance and satisfaction. The study found that poor management practices, such as lack of clear direction and feedback, failure to delegate responsibilities effectively, and ineffective communication, can lead to decreased employee morale and motivation. The result is decreased job *performance*, increased turnover intentions, and decreased overall job satisfaction.

Lau and Wood provide correlative insights into the detrimental effects of bad management on both employee job satisfaction and turnover intentions. The research, along with that of Robbins, Judge, & Sanghi, underscores the importance of fostering positive managerial practices to enhance overall employee well-being and reduce turnover within organizations. Just as exceptional management leads to positive outcomes like improved employee job performance and work engagement, poor management does the exact opposite, resulting in job dissatisfaction, job failure, and voluntary attrition.

2. MANAGER PROFICIENCY ASSESSMENT

All improvement requires change ...

and change is only achievable with actionable knowledge.

The difference between a competent manager and an exceptional manager lies in their respective levels of skill, leadership, and the impact they have on their team and organization. A competent manager is one who possesses the necessary skills, knowledge, and experience to fulfill the basic requirements of their managerial role. They can effectively handle routine tasks, ensure that processes are followed, and meet established performance standards. A competent manager is reliable and can maintain team stability, but their approach may be more focused on maintaining the status quo rather than driving significant innovation or change.

Exceptional management, on the other hand, goes beyond mere competence. An exceptional manager stands out due to their outstanding performance, skills, or qualities. Being exceptional implies going above and beyond the standard expectations, **demonstrating a level of excellence that distinguishes the person from others**. Exceptional individuals often show creativity, innovation, leadership, and a capacity to achieve remarkable results. Their contributions surpass what is typically considered good or satisfactory, leading to a notable impact on their work, team, or organization.

Managerial competence signifies meeting the expected standards, while exceptional performance involves surpassing those standards and making a notable, positive difference. Consider a sales manager overseeing a team responsible for meeting quarterly sales targets. A competent manager may ensure that their team follows established sales processes, meets individual quotas, and maintains a satisfactory level of client satisfaction. They successfully lead the team to achieve the baseline sales goals, but their approach may not involve significant strategic planning or transformative leadership.

On the other hand, an exceptional sales manager not only ensures the team meets targets but also introduces innovative sales strategies, mentors team members for personal and professional growth, and establishes strategic partnerships that lead to long-term business success. They go beyond the routine tasks of managing a sales team and actively contribute to the organization's overall growth and market positioning.

The implication of moving from competent to exceptional is that the manager must improve, and since all improvement requires change, the competent manager must do things differently than they have done and are doing today. Change is not possible without profound knowledge, suggesting that a first step in a manager going from competent to exceptional is to acquire knowledge about the manager's proficiency, their approach to the job, the impact of that approach, and their demonstrated level of competence, leadership, and achievement.

So, to determine the manager's current level of proficiency and what change is necessary for managerial improvement, some form of assessment is required. A managerial assessment is a structured evaluation or analysis of a manager's skills, competencies, and performance within the workplace. It typically involves the measurement of various managerial attributes, including leadership abilities, communication skills, decision-making capabilities, and other qualities relevant to effective management. Managerial assessments can take different forms, such as self-assessments, peer reviews, or evaluations conducted by higher-ups, and they aim to provide insights into a manager's strengths, areas for improvement, and overall effectiveness in their role. These assessments play a crucial role in talent development, succession planning, and organizational performance improvement.

My approach to the managerial assessment is the **Manager Proficiency Assessment (MPA)**. The MPA is an established method for enhancing managerial proficiency, beginning with a thorough assessment, serving as the conduit through which organizations gain essential insights. This systematic approach involves collecting evidence to gauge how well managers' performance aligns with expectations and standards. It encompasses the meticulous analysis and interpretation of this evidence, enabling us to generate information that can be used to document, elucidate, and enhance managerial performance to get the manager from where they are today to where the could or should be—an ideal state.

At a minimum, a manager proficiency assessment should include:

Conduct a pre-assessment planning session

The pre-assessment meeting is a meeting with the organization and project team leaders to discuss the Assessment effort, explain the methodology, discuss the support and logistical requirements from all parties, confirm the communication plan and approach, and ensure that the client has a solid understanding of all aspects of the Assessment effort. In addition, the planning team will articulate the desired outcomes of the Assessment and define the project's purpose, which will partly determine how the Assessment is conducted and reported.

Define the scope of the Assessment

Assessing every manager in large organizations—those with multiple locations in different countries, regions, and states, with tens-of-thousands of employees spread across different physical locations—can be challenging and resource-consuming; it can also be a waste of time and other resources. Most organizations choose to assess individual managers or a select group of managers based on the desired outcome of the effort.

To optimize the assessment data gathering effort for a group of managers, we recommend defining and assessing a "Representative Study Group." The *study group* (also known as the "sample group") is the group of managers whose proficiency will be analyzed in detail. A *representative* study group is a purposefully defined subset of the organization's managers that incorporates various job responsibility types, work process characteristics, and leadership behaviors found throughout the broader organization. The representative study group's findings and results are often extrapolated to represent the organization's *representative types* of managers in the total population.

Collect quantitative and qualitative data

As appropriate, gather qualitative and quantitative data through a combination of data-gathering approaches, including shadowing, in-person interviews, focus groups, on-site work process study, surveys, job descriptions, reports, and other methods as warranted.

Assess and analyze the data

Assessing and analyzing management study data involves a systematic examination of the collected information to extract meaningful insights and conclusions. The initial steps include validating the accuracy and reliability of the data, addressing any inconsistencies or errors, and coding information for structured analysis. Descriptive statistics are then generated to provide a summary of key management findings. Conduct comparative analysis to explore variations between different managers or groups, and correlation analysis which uncovers potential relationships between variables affecting managerial proficiency. Use the findings to infer predictions about the broader population based on the study group.

Perform a gap analysis

A gap analysis for a study of managerial proficiency involves a comparison of the current state of managerial skills competencies, and performance (the *benchmark*), against the desired or expected state. It depicts where a manager is today versus where the organization's leaders expect or want the manager to be. The process begins by defining the ideal set of managerial attributes and standards based on organizational goals, industry benchmarks, and best practices. Subsequently, the existing proficiency levels of managers are assessed through data collection methods referenced above. The identified gaps between the current and desired proficiency levels highlight areas where managers fall short or excel. These gaps serve as critical indicators, offering insights into the specific skills or competencies that need improvement to align with organizational objectives.

Present the findings and recommendations

The Findings & Recommendations report following the Manager Proficiency Assessment encompasses a thorough exploration of the current state of managerial skills and the proposed strategies for improvement. The report summarizes the assessment's objectives, methodologies, key findings, and recommendations to improve managerial proficiency. The core of the report lies in the recommendations section, presenting a comprehensive set of actionable strategies, training programs, and coaching initiatives tailored to address identified gaps. An implementation plan outlines the steps, responsibilities, and timeline for executing the proposed strategies, advancing a clear pathway for managerial improvement.

The Performance Lab's approach to the Manager Proficiency Assessment (MPA) is depicted below.

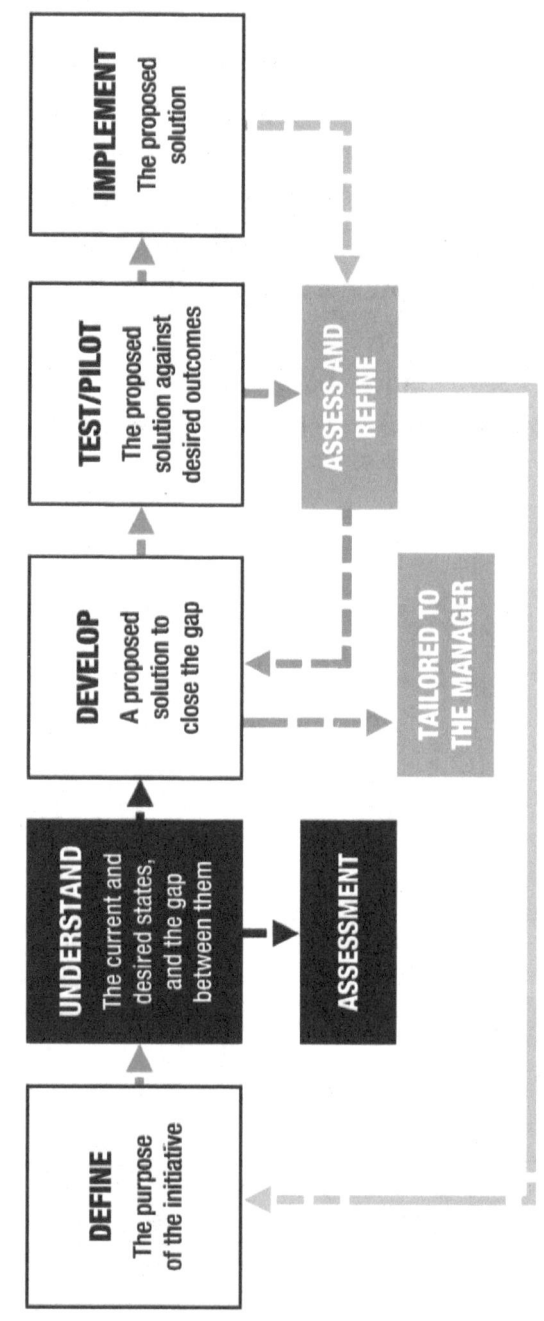

FROM COMPETENT TO EXCEPTIONAL

SYKL: Study managerial proficiency as a system

In my experience, when studying managerial proficiency, job performance, and organizational optimization, it is critical to assess the situation holistically. Leaders must have a deep understanding of the *systems* within which their managers operate.

"Systems thinking" plays a pivotal role in assessing an organization's managers' proficiency as it offers a holistic and interconnected perspective on various components within the organizational framework. Managers operate within a complex system where their actions and decisions have ripple effects on different facets of the organization. By employing systems thinking, assessors can understand the interdependencies and relationships among different managerial functions, recognizing that changes in one area may impact others. This approach helps avoid isolated evaluations and encourages a comprehensive analysis of how managers contribute to the overall effectiveness of the organization. Systems thinking fosters a deeper understanding of the managerial ecosystem, emphasizing that proficiency is not just about individual skills but also about how those skills integrate into the larger organizational context.

At The Performance Lab, we introduced *SYKL* (pronounced *cycle*), a cutting-edge approach to performance improvement rooted in systems thinking.

At its core, SYKL recognizes that all elements in an organization, including managerial performance, are interconnected, and the system of elements works as a whole to achieve team, department, functional area, operating unit, and overall organizational goals. Conceptually, organizations function as a **connected cycle of activity**, or "SYKL," with no clear beginning or end and require viewing organizational excellence as a continuous and ongoing process constantly evolving and adapting to internal and external changes. Through our SYKL approach, organizations can take a holistic view to understand managerial performance and proficiency, identifying the opportunity to adjust the right levers to achieve desired outcomes. This involves identifying the system's feedback loops, patterns, and relationships and making necessary adjustments. It is through a holistic approach such as SYKL that organization leaders can make more informed, actionable decisions that consider all of the impacts on managerial performance.

3. SAFETY

Providing safety, whether psychological or emotional, is critical for the manager, employee, team, and overall organizational success. In many cases, organizations may use these terms interchangeably or emphasize one over the other based on their specific goals and initiatives. Both concepts are crucial for fostering a positive and supportive workplace culture where individuals can thrive personally and professionally.

"Psychological safety" is a broader concept that encompasses creating an environment where individuals feel safe to express themselves, share ideas, and take interpersonal risks without fear of negative consequences. It goes beyond just emotions and includes the overall perception of safety in expressing diverse thoughts and opinions.

"Emotional safety" in an organization refers to the creation of a supportive and inclusive environment where employees feel secure expressing their thoughts, ideas, and emotions without fear of judgment, reprisal, or negative consequences. It involves fostering a workplace culture that values open communication, vulnerability, and mutual respect among team members.

For managers, providing safety is critical because it directly influences the overall well-being, engagement, and productivity of their teams. When employees feel psychologically and emotionally safe, they are more likely to share innovative ideas, collaborate effectively, and take calculated risks, leading to increased creativity and problem-solving within the team. The potential negative impact of not having emotional safety in a manager's department is a culture of fear and silence.

In an environment where employees are afraid to voice concerns or propose new ideas due to perceived consequences, innovation and creativity suffer. The lack of safety may lead to a stagnant work culture, diminished morale, and a decrease in employee engagement, hindering the team's overall performance.

> **A psychologically and emotionally safe environment promotes employee well-being, reducing stress and anxiety levels.**

On the flip side, when a manager actively fosters safety, teams experience numerous benefits. Firstly, it enhances trust among team members, promoting stronger collaboration and better communication. Team members are more likely to share their perspectives, which leads to a diversity of thought and solutions. Additionally, a safe environment **promotes employee well-being**, reducing stress and anxiety levels. This, in turn, positively impacts job satisfaction, employee retention, and overall team cohesion.

Creating a psychologically and emotionally safe environment as a manager involves intentional actions that foster trust, open communication, and a supportive workplace culture. Active listening is paramount. Managers should genuinely listen to their team members, acknowledging their concerns, ideas, and feelings without judgment. Demonstrating empathy and understanding builds a foundation of trust.

Promoting open communication channels is another key aspect. Managers can encourage team members to share their thoughts, even if they differ from the mainstream, and create platforms for open dialogue, such as regular team meetings or feedback sessions. This transparency helps in addressing issues proactively and preventing them from escalating.

Setting clear expectations and providing constructive feedback is essential. When team members understand their roles and receive feedback that **focuses on improvement rather than blame**, they feel supported and are more likely to contribute actively. Managers should also lead by example, showing vulnerability and admitting when they make mistakes. This openness creates a culture where everyone feels comfortable being authentic.

Recognizing and celebrating achievements, both big and small, contributes to a positive environment. Acknowledging individual and team accomplishments fosters a sense of appreciation and boosts morale. Also, providing resources for professional and personal development sends a message that the manager values the growth and well-being of their team members, reinforcing the notion that the workplace is invested in their success. In combination, these actions help cultivate a safe environment where employees feel heard, valued, and supported in their professional journey.

4. PERFORMANCE PLANNING

Strategy Alignment to the Performance Plan

As I collaborate with organizations and individuals across various regions, experiences reveal two primary reasons why the performance planning process between managers and employees is mostly ineffective: the lack of appreciation for strategic alignment and low-value progress review meetings.

When surveyed, a high percentage of managers claim to understand and could explain strategic alignment, and in most cases, they can. However, the issue lies in the fact that, while managers can articulate the concept of alignment, they seldom implement it in practice at the individual contributor level.

In a previous discussion, I explained how a strategy should incorporate cause-and-effect logic, where specific actions result in desired outcomes. For instance, if a salesperson's conversion rate is 9%, with each buyer spending an average of $100, then if the salesperson contacts 110 prospects, they will achieve their sales KPI of $1,000.

Revisiting the pizza example, the savvy pizza shop owners would break down the overarching goal of selling 300 pizzas into three equal parts, assigning each pizza manager the objective of selling 100 pizzas by week's end. Since most managers with people responsibilities rely on their employees to achieve KPIs, the pizza managers would cascade smaller KPIs down to their teams, incorporating them into each employee's annual performance plan. This ensures that employees understand the importance of KPI achievement, as it aligns with job performance, raises, promotions, etc. As a result, the employees would focus their daily efforts on selling the required number of pizzas, gaining a **clear line of sight into how their work contributes directly to the success of the pizza shop**. This visibility motivates employees and provides their job with meaning and purpose.

Alignment also motivates employees to work more productively by ensuring they spend their valuable work hours performing activities that will help them achieve their KPIs. In other words, the focused work activities of pizza employees (the cause) will result in pizza sales (the effect).

Two primary reasons why the performance planning process between managers and employees is mostly ineffective: the lack of appreciation for strategic alignment and low-value progress review meetings.

FROM COMPETENT TO EXCEPTIONAL

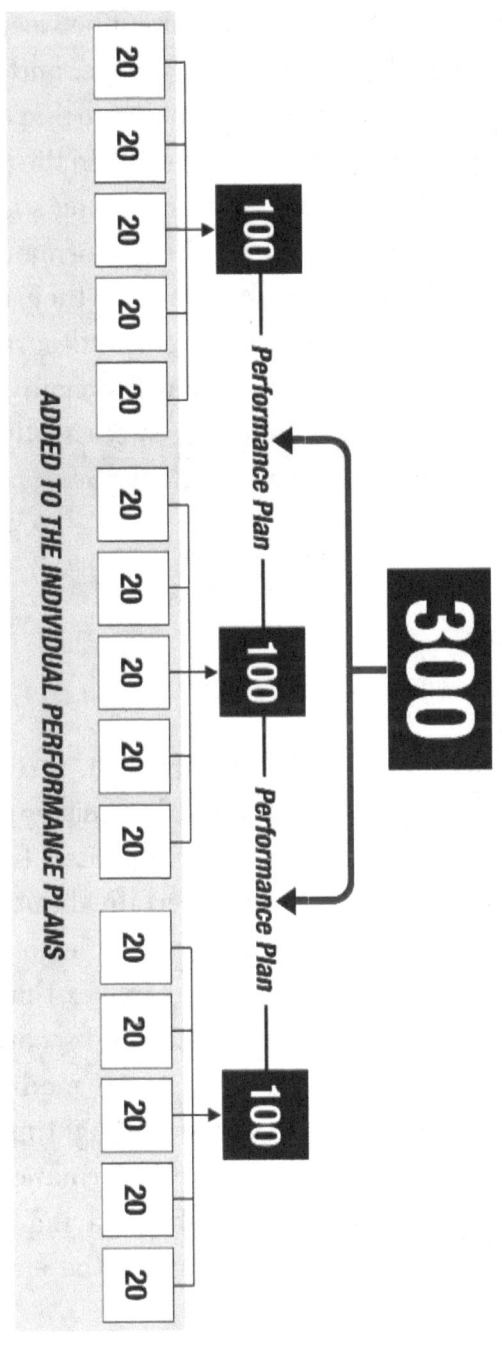

To create *meaningful* alignment between the organization's goals, the manager's goals, and the employees' goals, the manager must ensure that cause-and-effect logic exists organization-wide in the performance plans of the employees. When doing so, it is critical that the KPIs created for the performance plans are specific and measurable. Where they are not, the manager must gain alignment and agreement with the employees on how they will unequivocally determine whether the employee successfully achieved a KPI. This should be mandatory.

In January 2024, Brittany Pietsch, a recently hired accounts executive at the IT management services company Cloudflare, was terminated from her job. To this day, she remains uncertain about whether she was *laid off* due to business struggles or *fired* due to poor job performance. What makes this story noteworthy are two factors: firstly, she recorded the entire event and shared it on social media. Secondly, it serves as a clear example highlighting the importance of an employee's Key Performance Indicators being specific and measurable, leaving no room for ambiguity about the reasons for the employee's departure.

Upon receiving a 15-minute calendar invite with two human resources representatives she didn't know, similar to the invitations her coworkers received before being fired, Pietsch decided to record the interaction, later posting the nine-minute exchange on TikTok. In the video, one HR representative plainly stated that Pietsch was being let go because she had not met class expectations for performance. Interestingly, a Cloudflare spokesperson mentioned that 60 other individuals were dismissed *on the same day* for not meeting performance standards, raising questions about the extent of performance challenges being the reason for the terminations.

While some HR professionals watching the TikTok video speculated that Pietsch was *laid off*, they believed Cloudflare was attempting to disguise the separation as a *termination* to minimize exposure and provide minimal severance. Pietsch, visibly frustrated in the video, repeatedly requested tangible data behind the assessment of not meeting performance expectations, emphasizing her belief in doing a great job with impressive activity, meetings, and client relationships. The HR representatives, however, failed to provide specific, unambiguous, time-bound KPIs or metrics that led to her termination.

Such situations can lead to lawsuits between the employee and employer, with accusations of the employer's inability to articulate a specific performance-based reason for termination. Conversely, instances where a manager gives one employee a raise and a top performance rating based on ambiguous, subjective criteria can lead to accusations of favoritism, potentially impacting employee morale and engagement.

Progress Review Meetings

> 80% of monthly or periodic 1-on-1 progress reviews and meetings between the manager and employee are ineffective.

Why? Because the meetings do not accomplish the purpose for which they should be held: to make progress toward and ensure the employee's success. Periodic 1-on-1 meetings between the manager and direct report should focus on the employee's experience and achieving their job success in the current year.

The **employee experience** encompasses the entirety of an individual's interactions, perceptions, and feelings throughout their tenure within an organization. It begins with the initial stages of recruitment and onboarding, extending through their daily work responsibilities, interactions with colleagues and leadership, opportunities for professional development, and ultimately, their departure or advancement within the company. A positive employee experience prioritizes a supportive and inclusive workplace culture, meaningful work assignments, opportunities for growth, clear communication, and recognition for contributions. It considers the physical and virtual work environments, the relationships formed within the team, and the alignment between individual values and organizational goals. A well-crafted employee experience not only enhances job satisfaction and engagement but also plays a crucial role in talent retention and the overall success of the organization.

The *totality* of an employee's experience in a job is a key determinant of their performance and willingness to stay with an organization. Unfortunately, progress review meetings seldom consider an employee's total experience. Plus, the data show that constructive working sessions focused on the employee's progress toward achieving their periodic or annual KPIs seldom occur. Instead, these meetings are little more than "How ya doin'?" and "How's everything goin'?" conversations that do little-to-nothing toward strategically moving the employee forward toward a positive experience and successful year, where "success" is defined as achieving the employee's Key Performance Indicators.

The Action Feedback Loop

The most effective 1-on-1 periodic review meetings are intentional and adhere to a four-step format consistent with our *Action Feedback Loop* performance review model illustrated in the diagram below. The structured process includes:

1. A comprehensive review of the employee's Key Performance Indicators (KPIs) with a discussion of their **work activities and actions**, emphasizing their connection to progress and the achievement of KPIs.

2. Evaluation and discussion of the **measurable impact** generated by the employee's work activities, emphasizing quantifiable outcomes and the extent of their contribution to achieving the KPIs. We believe KPIs should be specific and measurable, ensuring clarity in assessing their accomplishment.

3. An in-depth review and discussion, essentially an **assessment**, of the employee's work activities and actions. This phase focuses on their impact (or lack thereof) on KPIs, leading to key learnings based on the effectiveness and significance of the employee's actions. Positive outcomes are celebrated, while areas lacking progress prompt adjustments for improvement.

4. Documentation of **necessary adjustments**. If the employee's activities and actions had no or a negative impact on achieving the KPIs, a course correction is recommended. This involves adapting the action plan, refining productivity practices, and adjusting work behaviors, all documented for clarity. These adjusted action items then become the focus of the next 1-on-1 meeting in the feedback loop.

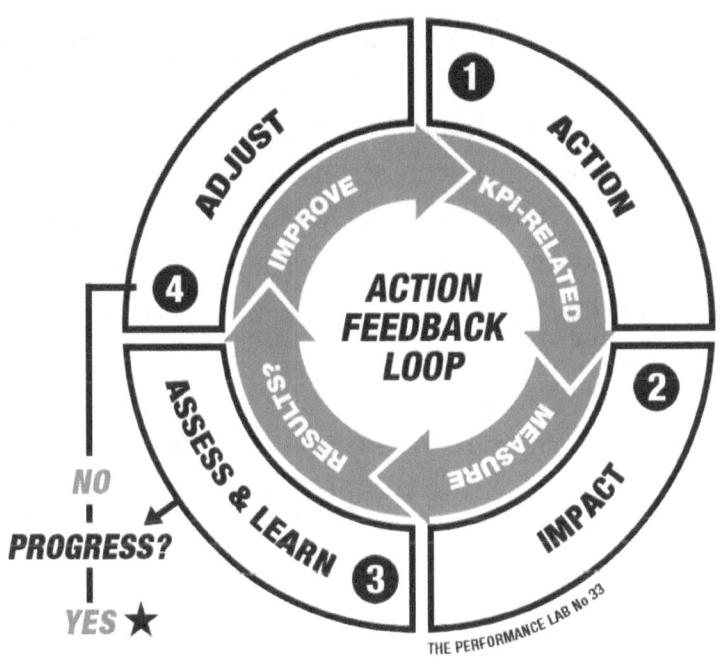

ON MANAGEMENT

Progress Review Meeting Best Practices

Conducting progress review meetings is critical for the effective management of projects, project-based work, and employee performance. These meetings provide a structured platform for assessing the current status of initiatives, identifying any challenges or roadblocks, and ensuring alignment with organizational goals. For projects, regular progress reviews help project managers and team members track milestones, evaluate timelines, and make necessary adjustments to stay on course. In the context of project-based work, these meetings facilitate collaboration, enhance communication, and ensure that individual contributions contribute cohesively to the project's success.

The following best-practices, as the name implies, have been proven to improve the overall effectiveness and value of progress and periodic review meetings between the manager and employee.

- **Calendared, planned, and structured (agenda):** Scheduling and calendaring recurring, periodic 1-on-1 meetings between managers and employees offer several benefits for effective communication and relationship-building within the workplace. These scheduled sessions provide a consistent and structured platform for ongoing discussions, fostering open dialogue about work progress, challenges, and goals. Regular 1-on-1 meetings create a sense of accountability, allowing both managers and employees to track individual and team objectives, address concerns, and strategize for success.

- **Peer accountability partner:** A peer accountability partner is a trusted colleague who collaborates with you to support mutual goal achievement, providing encouragement, feedback, and shared responsibility for maintaining commitment and progress.

- **The use of a scorecard:** A progress scorecard is a visual or documented representation that tracks and measures the progress of specific objectives or key performance indicators (KPIs) over a defined period. It serves as a tool for evaluating and communicating the advancement toward set goals, allowing individuals or teams to assess their performance against predetermined benchmarks.

- **Productivity support tool (e.g., email, calendar)**

- **Employee self-assessment:** An employee self-assessment is a reflective process in which an individual evaluates their own performance, accomplishments, strengths, and areas for improvement within their job role, typically as part of a performance appraisal or review.

- **Incorporate the KPI *Action Feedback Loop***
- **Focus on KPIs or desired outcomes:** Any activity in which a manager or employee engages that is not in direct support of accomplishing a KPI, goal, or achieving an objective is wasted effort.
- **Milestone "rewards":** providing milestone rewards is a strategic approach to recognizing and reinforcing positive behaviors, fostering a culture of achievement, and ultimately contributing to a motivated, engaged, and high-performing workforce.
- **Facilitate solutions vs. prescribing them:** Facilitating a solution involves guiding and supporting team members in identifying and implementing their own resolutions to challenges. It emphasizes collaborative problem-solving, where the manager acts as a facilitator, encouraging open communication and leveraging the collective intelligence of the team. This approach promotes employee autonomy, fosters a sense of ownership, and encourages creativity in problem-solving.

  On the other hand, prescribing solutions entails a more directive role for the manager, where they provide a specific answer or course of action to address a problem. While this approach may be appropriate in certain situations, it can limit employees' growth, inhibit innovation, and create a dependency on the manager for solutions.

- **Ask vs. tell – but try to avoid asking "Why?"**
When a manager asks, they seek input, opinions, or suggestions from team members, fostering a collaborative environment where diverse perspectives are valued. This approach encourages employee engagement, promotes creativity, and can lead to more informed decisions. On the other hand, when a manager tells, they provide clear instructions or directives without soliciting input, often in a more authoritarian manner. While telling may be necessary in certain situations, such as urgent matters or when clear guidance is required, it can limit employee autonomy and stifles opportunities for shared decision-making.

    Asking "why?" in a manager-employee conversation or review can be a delicate matter. While the intention might be to gain a deeper understanding of the employee's actions, decisions, or performance, the manner in which "why?" is posed can inadvertently create a defensive or confrontational atmosphere. Employees may perceive it as a challenge to justify their actions, leading to discomfort or resistance.

    The problem arises when the question is framed in a way that seems accusatory or judgmental, rather than genuinely seeking clarification or insights. To navigate this issue effectively, managers should consider framing questions in a more open and neutral manner, fostering a constructive dialogue that encourages employees to share their perspectives without feeling defensive.

- **An opportunity to strengthen the relationship:** One-on-one meetings between managers and employees serve as a crucial platform for strengthening the relationship and fostering emotional safety within the workplace. These meetings provide a dedicated space for open and honest communication, allowing both parties to share their thoughts, concerns, and aspirations. A manager can use this time to actively listen to the employee's perspectives, acknowledge their contributions, and address any challenges they may be facing. By demonstrating empathy and understanding, managers create a supportive environment that promotes trust and psychological safety.

   Moreover, these meetings are an opportunity for managers to provide constructive feedback, recognizing achievements and offering guidance for improvement. Constructive feedback delivered in a positive and encouraging manner contributes to the employee's professional development and reinforces a culture of continuous improvement. Additionally, discussing career goals, aspirations, and skill development during these sessions helps employees feel valued and supported in their professional journey.

Incorporating elements of mentorship and coaching into one-on-one meetings further enhances the manager-employee relationship. Managers can offer guidance, share experiences, and provide resources to help employees thrive in their roles. This collaborative approach not only strengthens the professional bond but also contributes to the overall well-being and job satisfaction of the employee. Creating a space where employees feel heard, respected, and supported ultimately contributes to the establishment of emotional safety within the workplace.

Giving Feedback

> "Feedback" is a discussion centered on the opportunity for achieving excellence.

Feedback between a manager and employee refers to the communication and exchange of information regarding the employee's performance, behavior, or accomplishments in the workplace. It is a process where the manager provides insights, observations, and constructive comments to the employee based on their work, with the aim of fostering improvement, growth, and alignment with organizational goals.

This feedback can encompass various aspects, including the employee's strengths, areas for improvement, and specific behaviors impacting their performance. Effective feedback is typically timely, specific, and actionable, providing the employee with clear guidance on how to enhance their performance or skills. Additionally, feedback should **be a two-way communication**, allowing employees to share their perspectives, ask questions, and seek clarification, contributing to a more collaborative and development-oriented work environment.

The primary purpose of feedback is to facilitate growth, development, and improvement. Or, as I believe, feedback should be a discussion centered on **the opportunity for achieving excellence**. Unfortunately, as our work shows, 99% of managers provide employee feedback and conduct feedback sessions poorly.

> **Feedback, the way it is provided by most managers, is mostly criticism.**

The problems with feedback

Why are managers so ineffective at giving feedback that drives excellence? The reasons are many, including (but not limited to):

- **Humans are unreliable raters of other humans, yet we think we are reliable:** This problem stems from overconfidence in our ability to accurately assess others. Despite being inherently subjective and prone to biases, individuals often believe in their objectivity when evaluating the performance of their peers or subordinates.

- **Human biases come into play:** Bias is a pervasive challenge in feedback. Various biases, such as affinity bias or confirmation bias, can unconsciously influence the way feedback is given and received. This hinders the objective evaluation of performance and can lead to unfair assessments.

- **We can only reliably tell someone, for example, that their presentation is boring to us, but not in general:** Feedback is often limited to personal preferences and subjective opinions, making it challenging to provide universally applicable insights. What may be perceived as boring by one person might be engaging for another.

ON MANAGEMENT

- **People are unreliable on rating others on abstract and subjective attributes like potential, creative thinking, and being a team player:** Evaluating abstract and subjective qualities introduces further complexity. Attributes like potential or creativity are challenging to quantify objectively, making it difficult to provide accurate and constructive feedback in these areas.

- **Focusing people on their shortcomings doesn't enable learning; it impairs it:** Emphasizing weaknesses rather than strengths can hinder the learning process. Constructive feedback should strike a balance, highlighting areas for improvement while recognizing and leveraging an individual's strengths.

- **People do not do well when someone whose intentions are unclear tells us where we stand and what we must do to fix ourselves:** Lack of clarity in feedback delivery can create confusion and anxiety. Unclear intentions or vague guidance may lead to a lack of understanding about the necessary steps for improvement.

- **The human brain is wired to run away from threats; we perceive negative feedback as a threat:** Negative feedback triggers the brain's threat response, leading to defensive reactions. This can impede the receptiveness of individuals to feedback, hindering the potential for constructive learning and improvement.

- **We think we are better than we are:** Overestimating one's abilities is a common cognitive bias. Individuals may resist feedback that challenges their self-perception, creating a barrier to acknowledging and addressing areas for improvement.
- **"Safety" and fear of retaliation:** In some organizational cultures, there may be a pervasive fear among employees that providing honest feedback, especially if it's critical, could lead to negative consequences such as retaliation, discrimination, or damage to professional relationships.

Toward improving the feedback dynamic

The prevalence of criticism in contemporary feedback processes can be attributed to several factors within the organizational and managerial domains. Traditional performance evaluation models often focus on identifying and rectifying shortcomings rather than emphasizing strengths and achievements. Managers, guided by these models, may feel compelled to highlight areas for improvement, inadvertently framing feedback predominantly in a critical light. This approach stems from a historical perspective that **views feedback as a means of addressing deficiencies rather than nurturing an individual's potential**.

Moreover, organizational cultures that prioritize a fixed mindset, where abilities are perceived as innate and unchangeable, tend to foster a feedback environment centered around criticism. In such settings, individuals may be hesitant to embrace constructive feedback, fearing it as a judgment on their inherent capabilities rather than an opportunity for growth. This mindset perpetuates a cycle where managers predominantly provide critical feedback, reinforcing a culture that may hinder professional development.

Shifting towards a more constructive and growth-oriented feedback approach involves adopting a mindset that views feedback as a catalyst for improvement, focusing not just on weaknesses but also on strengths and potential. Encouraging open communication, emphasizing employee development, and fostering a positive feedback culture are essential steps in breaking away from the cycle of feedback-as-criticism.

To shift the focus of feedback from criticism to a more constructive and excellence-driven approach, managers can adopt several key strategies. For starters, it is essential to **reframe the purpose of feedback**, emphasizing its role in fostering growth, learning, and overall improvement rather than merely pointing out shortcomings. This shift in mindset creates a foundation for a more positive and developmental feedback culture.

Managers should strive to provide feedback that is specific, actionable, and future-oriented. Instead of dwelling solely on what went wrong, they can highlight specific achievements and strengths, reinforcing positive behaviors that contribute to success. This approach empowers employees by acknowledging their capabilities and encouraging them to leverage their strengths in achieving excellence.

Additionally, feedback sessions should be viewed as collaborative discussions rather than one-sided evaluations. Managers can engage employees in setting goals, identifying areas for improvement, and jointly creating action plans. This collaborative approach fosters a sense of ownership and commitment, making employees more receptive to feedback as they actively participate in their professional development. However, this must be done in a psychologically and emotionally **safe environment**.

Recognizing and reinforcing positive behaviors and accomplishments helps build confidence and motivates employees to strive for excellence. Ultimately, a shift toward a feedback model focused on achieving excellence requires a cultural transformation that values growth, learning, and the collective success of both individuals and the organization.

ENABLING EXCELLENCE

After nine seasons of failure, former Dallas Cowboys football coach Tom Landry led his team to success by focusing on his players' strengths rather than their mistakes.

Landry focused his players' attention on little things that they had done well. The idea was to capture the distinctive moments of excellence and enable the individual players to learn how to repeat them.

5. PRODUCTIVITY

A meaningful discussion about work efficiency and productivity cannot commence without establishing the context in which these terms will apply throughout this book. Broadly, "productivity" refers to the efficiency with which resources or inputs, such as labor and capital (including Human Capital), are converted into outputs of goods and services or lead to the achievement of some other desired outcome or end-product, like a goal. To *produce* is to bring something into existence, to fruition, using the resources available at one's disposal. **Productivity** is, therefore, the degree to which one can produce a predefined result or achieve a goal, objective, or other desired outcome while considering the impact on resources. **In the workplace, productivity practically means completing activities that bring you closer to achieving a work objective or other Key Performance Indicator.**

Increased productivity implies that more output can be produced, and greater success can be achieved using the same or fewer inputs or resources, allowing workers to enjoy higher living standards, such as improved health and well-being, education, and environmental conditions. This is what motivates employers to help employees increase their work productivity.

Engaging in *productive* work—work that directly contributes to a desirable end product, outcome, or result—leads to **job success;** it involves accomplishing significant tasks. In this context, "significant" (or *priority* or *critical)* pertains to activities that, when completed, bring the worker closer to achieving an objective or other desired outcome. It also encompasses work that carries unfavorable consequences if left incomplete, even if the tasks themselves don't directly contribute to the worker's objectives or Key Performance Indicators.

What is essential to understand about productivity is that being productive is not synonymous with quality; it only means that one has fundamentally produced or achieved some desired outcome.

> **In the workplace, productivity practically means completing activities that bring you closer to achieving a work objective or other Key Performance Indicator.**

Measuring Productivity

A basic equation for productivity is structured as follows:

$$\text{PRODUCTIVITY} = \left(\frac{\text{OUTCOME OR BENEFIT}}{\text{COST OF THE ACHIEVEMENT}} \right)$$

When applying this formula to measure the productivity of an activity, such as completing an action item, or the application of an asset, like money, a resulting value of "1" or higher implies that the application of that resource has been positive or productive. It indicates that the overall return on the investment of a resource (time, effort, money, human capital, equipment, means of production, and similar resources) has yielded a favorable result or outcome. A resulting value of less than "1," however, is unfavorable and implies that the cost of achieving the outcome or producing the benefit exceeds the value of the outcome or benefit, making it a bad investment. In other words, the productivity value from this equation suggests that the higher the "cost" of achieving an outcome or benefit, the lower the degree of productivity of the activity or asset. For instance, if the desired outcome is the completion of a project, and the resource cost (e.g., work hours) required to complete the project, projected to take two days, takes an employee three weeks, the project, while ultimately completed, would be considered an unproductive or wasteful activity.

Favorable productivity is a function of efficiency (performing an activity or function with the least waste of effort and resources, like time, labor, capital, etc.) and effectiveness (adeptness at achieving expected results). Combined, they form the basis of reliable job performance, something all managers seek for their employees. Measuring productivity using methods or tools as simple as the previously referenced productivity equation can not only provide insight into whether an activity or resource is productive or unproductive but also allow for the measurement of degrees of productivity, enabling the comparison of the relative measures of productivity in multiple situations.

Suppose, for example, that a company hired two people, Bob and Ken, to perform the same job: build a wooden doghouse to sell in pet stores. The company agreed to pay each builder $25 per hour worked; it is expected to take 4 hours for each person to build a doghouse at a total cost of $100 each. The objective is to sell the doghouses for $150 each, making a nice $50 profit on the sale of each house. When the builders began building the doghouses, Bob completed his house in the expected 4 hours, while it took Ken 5 hours to complete the construction of his doghouse.

In the strictest sense, both Bob and Ken could be considered to have productively built their respective doghouses because they both engaged in work activities that led to the desired outcome: a sellable doghouse. The company can calculate the workers' basic productivity by applying the metrics of the case to the productivity equation:

Bob: Productivity = [$150 doghouse/$100 cost] = 1.5
Ken: Productivity = [$150 doghouse/$125 cost] = 1.2

This calculation illustrates how both Bob and Ken could be considered to have productively built the doghouses because, per the equation, each man received a productivity score greater than "1." It also illustrates that Bob worked more productively than Ken, having achieved a productivity score of 1.5 vs. 1.2. However, when we consider whether each man performed his job *successfully*—with "success" defined as building a sellable $150 doghouse in 4 hours at the cost of $100—only Bob did so.

In this example, only Bob was *favorably productive* because he performed his work activities in a manner that produced the desired outcome: not merely building a doghouse but doing so in 4 hours at the cost of $100. This nuanced idea of being productive versus favorably productive relates to the statement made previously, that being productive is not synonymous with efficiency; it only means that one has fundamentally produced or achieved some desired outcome. Ken built a doghouse, so he was productive at delivering the primary outcome. Bob, however, built a doghouse successfully by producing the essential outcome, the doghouse, and achieving the associated objective: building the $150 doghouse in 4 hours at the cost of $100.

The difference between being productive and favorably productive is nuanced. For this book, the term *productivity* is used to represent *favorable* productivity: completing relevant work that leads to the achievement of a goal, objective, or other desirable outcomes.

Measuring the costs and benefits of productivity is valuable for establishing a benchmark of the current level of these measures in an endeavor. This benchmark enables the measuring organization to gauge the impact of specific improvement initiatives, such as training, on the performance of its workers, considering both time-related ("soft") costs and currency-related ("hard") costs.

For example, an agency aimed to have its overworked staff spend more time at home with their families and friends and reduce overtime at work. Each of the salaried (not hourly) staff members worked an average of 10 hours each day. To help the staff work fewer hours while still meeting the daily requirement of widgets, the agency provided productivity training for the staff, costing $5,000 to train its team of 50 workers.

Before the workshop, the workers produced the required total of 1,000 widgets each day. After the workshop, however, the workers still produced the required 1,000 widgets but did so by working an average of only 8 hours each day; the training enabled the workers to accomplish the same amount of work in fewer hours.

To gauge the benefits and return on their investment in the training workshop, the agency's owner performed a cost-benefit analysis and calculated the training's Return on Investment (ROI). ROI is a performance measure used to evaluate the efficiency and benefit (or return) of an investment, represented as a simple ratio of the gain from an investment relative to its cost. The formula for calculating ROI is:

$$ROI = \left(\frac{\text{NET RETURN ON INVESTMENT}}{\text{COST OF THE INVESTMENT}}\right) \times 100\%$$

The table below provides the metrics for the agency and the resulting ROI.

Variable	Before the Training	After the Training
Number of daily widgets produced	1,000	1,000
Total daily hours needed to produce the widgets	500	400
Total daily work hours saved	--	**100**
Widgets produced per hour	2	2.5
Percentage increase in daily widget production	--	**25%**
Daily widget sales revenue (at $10 per widget)	$10,000	$10,000
Daily labor cost (at an average hourly-equivalent fully loaded worker salary of $35)	$17,500	$14,000
Daily productivity cost savings ("soft" costs)	--	$3,500
First-week productivity cost savings ("soft" costs)	--	$17,500
Cost of productivity training	--	($5,000)
Net cost savings from the productivity training	--	**$12,500**
Return on Investment from the training*	--	**250%**

* The training ROI is based on the time workers saved as a result of the training. I converted the time savings to a dollar amount. Since the workers are salaried, the agency did not save any "hard" or spendable dollars on labor costs; as salaried workers, they get paid the same whether they work 40 hours or 70 hours. Additionally, since the agency did not sell any additional widgets, they did not generate additional revenue as a result of the training. Therefore, the ROI calculation solely relies on the "soft," time-based costs related to the time saved by the workers.

$$ROI = \left(\frac{\text{NET BENEFIT OF THE TRAINING } (\$17{,}500 - \$5{,}000)}{\text{COST OF THE TRAINING } (\$5{,}000)} \right) \times 100\% = 250\%$$

One could argue that by working fewer daily hours, employees may accrue ancillary benefits such as less stress, more leisure time, and better overall well-being, resulting in lower healthcare costs, fewer sick days away from work, and other financial benefits. However, for this simple example, those factors were excluded.

As this example illustrates, the calculation of soft dollars can be useful in determining the relative improvement in a time-based process or activity. This example also implies that if an actual process exists, the firm must be able to map the process; as the saying goes: If you cannot map a work or workflow process, then you do not have a process. An added benefit of being able to map a process is that mapping will allow you to measure the stages and performance of the process, further enabling you to create a current-state benchmark of the process in question. That benchmark state would serve as the basis for determining whether or not corrective action has had an impact on the productivity of a worker, a process, or a system.

Productivity is Simple

Working productively is conceptually simple; it merely requires a commitment to becoming more productive, a willingness to work differently, discipline, and the minimization of distractions and interruptions. The productivity process is rather straightforward:

1. **Start with a purpose.** In the workplace, an employee's purpose is normally the successful achievement of KPIs. Retrieve your performance plan, document your objectives or KPIs, and make them visible daily. Your work objectives should dictate your primary work activities.

2. **Identify the tasks necessary to achieve the objectives.** Everyone's daily task list consists of various types of tasks: priority, important, non-urgent, and those with little to no importance. Separate those tasks that will lead to the achievement of your KPIs and add them to your priority task list. From the remaining tasks, extract those that hold negative consequences if not completed, and add those to the priority task list. Spend the majority of your time completing these activities. When completing your priority tasks, seek to minimize distractions and interruptions from your phone, email, other people, and wasteful meetings & conference calls.

3. **Allocate time on your calendar to complete your priority tasks.** Your calendar should contain priorities and important tasks to be completed. After you determine that a task is a priority or is important, allocate a day and time on your calendar to complete it, and maintain the discipline to work through your calendar, completing tasks on the day and time you intended to complete them.

4. **Complete the tasks as scheduled on your calendar.** After you complete your calendared priority & important tasks, check to ensure that they contributed to the achievement of an associated KPI or that you have mitigated any consequences by completing tasks that held consequences if not completed.

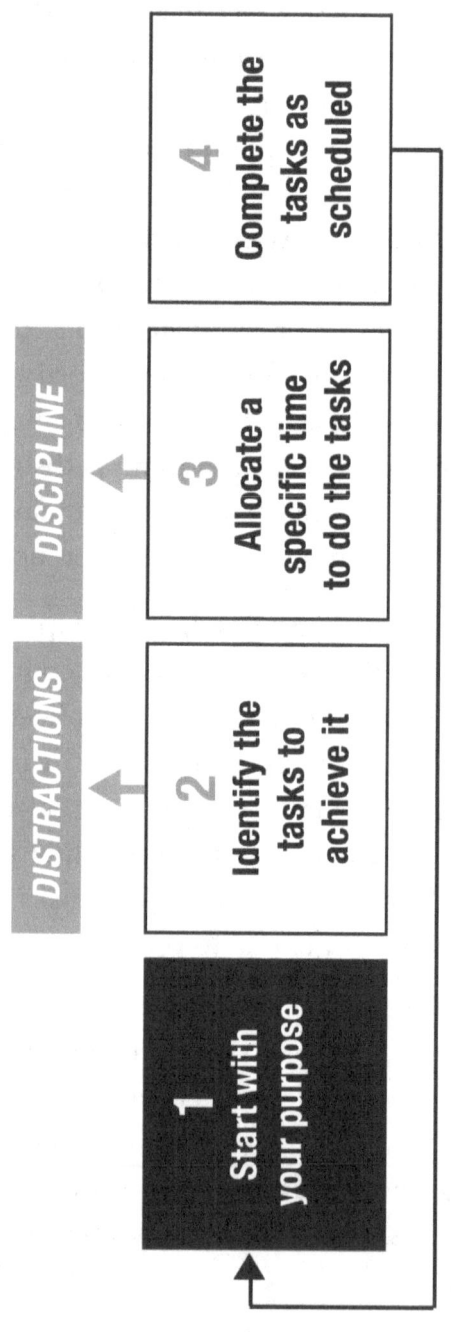

Micromanagement

In 1964, during the case of *Jacobellis v. Ohio*, United States Supreme Court Justice Potter Stewart faced the challenge of defining *obscenity*. The specific question was related to whether the French film "The Lovers" was obscene and not protected by the First Amendment. In his concurring opinion, Justice Stewart famously struggled to provide a precise definition of pornography or obscenity, stating, "I shall not today attempt further to define the kinds of material I understand to be embraced within that shorthand description, and perhaps I could never succeed in intelligibly doing so. But I know it when I see it, and the motion picture involved in this case is not that."

Describing "micromanagement" often poses a challenge for managers and employees alike, reminiscent of Justice Stewart's struggle. Ultimately, both parties arrive at a shared understanding of what micromanagement entails: "I know it when I see it." Regardless of their specific definitions, both managers and employees concur that it is undesirable. Managers generally believe they do not engage in it, while employees universally disdain it.

> **Micromanagement: I know it when I see it.**

Micromanagement is a management style characterized by excessive control, close supervision, and an overemphasis on minute details of tasks and processes. In a micromanaging approach, managers closely monitor and direct every aspect of their employees' work, often to an extent that hinders autonomy and creativity. This management style is marked by a lack of trust in employees' abilities and a desire for strict oversight.

Micromanagers may involve themselves deeply in day-to-day operations, leading to reduced morale, stifled innovation, and diminished employee engagement. The negative impact of micromanagement can result in decreased productivity and job satisfaction within a team or organization.

Micromanagement negatively impacts an employee's productivity due to several interconnected factors. First, micromanagement erodes trust between the manager and the employee. When a manager scrutinizes and controls every aspect of an employee's work, it signals a lack of confidence in the employee's abilities. This constant oversight can lead to feelings of frustration, disempowerment, and a diminished sense of ownership in the assigned tasks.

Secondly, micromanagement disrupts the natural flow of work and stifles creativity and innovation. Employees need a degree of autonomy to explore different approaches, make decisions, and find solutions. Micromanaging restricts this freedom, creating an environment where employees may become risk-averse or hesitant to take initiative, as they fear immediate criticism or intervention. Moreover, micromanagement consumes valuable time and resources. Managers who excessively involve themselves in minute details divert their attention from more strategic and high-priority tasks. This not only hampers the manager's effectiveness but also leaves employees waiting for approvals or feedback, leading to delays in project completion.

While micromanagement is generally perceived as detrimental, there are situations where it can be useful and even beneficial. For some managers, employing a more hands-on approach can be a sign of their power and confidence in leadership roles, showcasing their strong leadership abilities. When managers are highly involved and engaged in the details of projects, it can ensure a better understanding of the team's dynamics and foster a sense of unity. Acting as an extra set of eyes, micromanagers may foresee and prevent negative events, contributing to risk mitigation. In certain scenarios, micromanagement can facilitate employees' movement in a new direction, aiding in their professional growth. Moreover, for complex tasks, a micromanager can add value by leveraging their experience and providing guidance and support to those who may benefit from their expertise, fostering a collaborative and developmental work environment.

Research shows that when employees get hands-on managerial support, they perform better than when they are left to their own devices, but *unnecessary* or *unwanted* help can be counterproductive.

Fear

There are many causes of micromanagement, including a lack of trust in a subordinate's capabilities and a lack of patience for instance. But, in my experience, there is one factor that encompasses multiple reasons: fear.

Micromanagement often stems from a fundamental cause rooted in fear, and this fear can manifest in various ways within a manager's psyche. Fear of failure is a pervasive factor—managers, driven by a desire for success, may worry that any lapse in control could lead to suboptimal outcomes, damaging their reputation or standing within the organization. This fear might emerge from a competitive work environment where success is highly valued and perceived as the only acceptable outcome. Additionally, fear of losing control is a powerful motivator for micromanagers. They may believe that maintaining close oversight is the key to ensuring tasks are executed precisely as they envision. This fear can be intensified by a lack of trust in the team's abilities or concerns about their own job security. Micromanagers may worry that relinquishing control could lead to mistakes or deviations from their expectations, further fueling their impulse to closely monitor every detail.

Ultimately, the fear-based micromanagement dynamic reflects a manager's **internal anxieties** about uncertainty, failure, or a loss of control. Addressing these underlying fears and fostering a culture of trust can be pivotal in transforming micromanagement into a more collaborative and empowering leadership style.

To overcome the urge to micromanage, managers can adopt a more empowering and trust-based leadership approach. First and foremost, clear communication is essential. Establishing open and transparent communication channels builds trust between managers and employees. Setting clear expectations and goals allows employees to understand their roles, fostering a sense of autonomy. Encouraging a culture of accountability and providing support when needed reinforces the idea that managers trust their team members to handle responsibilities.

Delegation is a crucial aspect of relinquishing micromanagement tendencies. Managers should recognize the strengths and capabilities of their team members and assign tasks accordingly. Empowering employees to take ownership of their work not only builds confidence within the team but also allows managers to focus on strategic aspects of their role.

Furthermore, managers can foster a positive work environment by recognizing and celebrating achievements. Regular feedback sessions provide an opportunity for constructive discussions and mutual growth. By demonstrating confidence in their team's abilities, managers can break free from the micromanagement cycle, creating a more collaborative and productive work atmosphere.

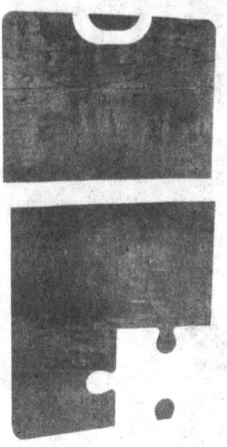

CHAPTER FOUR
THE MANAGEMENT JOURNEY

How does one ascend to a managerial role within an organization? What constitutes a typical trajectory for individual contributors aspiring to become managers? In numerous organizations, particularly larger enterprises, the journey toward a managerial position follows a structured course. Reflecting on my tenure as a sales representative at IBM, the process was methodical: excel in sales training for a year, achieve two successful years in account sales, progress to a support staff role for two years, and finally, attain a managerial position. This progression was almost predictable, and a successful IBM sales representative could anticipate reaching a managerial role within five or six years. However, it's crucial to note that this specific road-to-manager model at IBM concluded many years ago.

While the path to management varies due to factors like organizational size, business needs, attrition rates leading to new opportunities, and industry context, a discernible model emerges from these variations. Our research indicates several key stages that an employee may traverse on their journey to becoming an effective manager. This trajectory commences with individual contributors aspiring to managerial roles and progresses through various levels, ultimately reaching executive positions.

① Entry-Level Work	② Special Assignments	③ Skill Development	④ Early Management Roles
⑤ Learning the Job	⑥ Mid-Level Management	⑦ Hi-Po Candidate	⑧ Executive Leadership

I. **Entry-Level Work**: Starting at the ground level of an organization helps individuals understand the fundamental operations, processes, and culture of the company. This stage allows for learning by doing and grasping the basics of the business.

II. **Special Assignments**: Special assignments play an important role in accelerating an employee's transition into a managerial role by providing valuable experiential learning and a platform to **showcase leadership potential**. These assignments often expose individuals to challenges beyond their regular job responsibilities, offering a taste of the complexities associated with managerial roles. Special assignments can take various forms, such as leading a cross-functional project, managing a team for a specific initiative, or spearheading a critical organizational task. By engaging in such assignments, employees not only gain hands-on experience in decision-making, problem-solving, and strategic planning but also develop essential leadership skills. These experiences offer a practical understanding of the broader organizational context, fostering adaptability and a comprehensive view of managerial responsibilities.

Successful completion of special assignments signals to both the employee and organizational leadership that the individual is ready for more significant managerial responsibilities, expediting the transition process and enhancing the likelihood of a successful managerial career.

III. **Skill Development**: Employees typically undergo skill development through on-the-job experiences, training programs, workshops, or additional education (such as an MBA or specialized courses). This stage is crucial for honing technical skills relevant to their field and acquiring leadership abilities.

IV. **Early Management Roles**: Progressing to roles with more responsibilities, such as team leader or supervisor, helps individuals learn how to manage and coordinate a team's efforts. This stage involves understanding the dynamics of team communication, conflict resolution, and basic managerial tasks.

V. **Learning the job**: There is a proverb that states: "making mistakes is the best teacher." The rationale behind this statement is rooted in the belief that errors and failures provide invaluable learning opportunities. When individuals make mistakes, they are confronted with the consequences of their actions, gaining insights into what went wrong and why. This firsthand experience creates a deeper understanding of the task at hand, fosters critical thinking, and encourages **problem-solving skills**. The idea is that the lessons learned from making mistakes are often more memorable and impactful than simply receiving guidance or instructions. Embracing and learning from mistakes can lead to personal growth, resilience, and the development of a more robust skill set, ultimately contributing to long-term success.

VI. **Mid-Level Management**: As employees gain experience, they may advance to mid-level management positions. Here, they focus more on strategic planning, decision-making, and overseeing multiple teams or departments.

VII. **Hi-Po Candidate:** A "hi-po" manager, short for high-potential manager, refers to individuals recognized for their capacity, skills, and qualities that position them for success and progression into leadership roles within an organization. These high-potential employees, including managers, exhibit outstanding performance, leadership potential, and a keen ability for growth and development. The journey to becoming a hi-po manager typically entails a combination of factors such as performance excellence, leadership skills, continuous learning, adaptability, strategic thinking, networking and relationship building, and **demonstrated potential** for higher roles. Importantly, achieving the status of a high-potential manager is not a self-determined designation; rather, hi-po candidates are typically identified and selected by high-level managers within an organization.

VIII. **Executive Leadership:** The highest level of management involves strategic thinking, long-term planning, and setting the overall direction for the company. Executives often need to possess a holistic view of the business and industry, as well as exceptional leadership and decision-making skills.

Throughout these stages, individuals might also benefit from mentorship, continuous learning, and exposure to different aspects of the business to round out their managerial capabilities. Adaptability, communication, emotional intelligence, and the ability to motivate and inspire others are key attributes that evolve and become increasingly crucial at higher managerial levels.

Education and Training for Managerial Effectiveness

Based on research, a college education can positively impact a person's managerial effectiveness, but it is not the only factor. Many studies have shown that a higher education, particularly in business or management fields, can provide individuals with the theoretical knowledge, technical skills, and problem-solving abilities needed to succeed as managers. However, other factors such as work experience, leadership skills, and personal qualities such as emotional intelligence, communication skills, and integrity also play a crucial role in determining a manager's effectiveness.

Additionally, research has shown that a higher education alone may not necessarily lead to better management performance, as there is often a gap between what is taught in the classroom and the practicalities of real-world management. Furthermore, some research has indicated that managers with formal education may struggle with certain aspects of managing people, such as conflict resolution and employee motivation, due to a lack of hands-on experience.

While a college education can contribute to a person's managerial effectiveness, it should not be seen as the sole determinant of success. A combination of education, training, work experience, and personal qualities is likely to produce the most effective managers.

> **While a college education can contribute to a person's managerial effectiveness, it should not be seen as the sole determinant of success.**

There are numerous instances of accomplished managers who lack a college degree. Richard Branson, the visionary behind Virgin Group, left school at 16 and crafted a prosperous career as a business magnate and entrepreneur. Michael Dell, the founder and CEO of Dell Technologies, abandoned college to establish his computer company, transforming it into one of the globe's premier technology firms. Even Oprah Winfrey, the renowned media executive, television host, actress, and philanthropist, departed Tennessee State University to pursue a media career, emerging as one of the most successful and influential figures in the entertainment industry.

This prompts the question: what kinds of education and training best equip individual contributors to thrive in managerial roles?

Various types of formal education and training can significantly enhance managerial effectiveness by providing valuable skills and knowledge. For instance, courses in cost accounting can equip managers with a deep understanding of financial principles, enabling them to make informed decisions about resource allocation and budgeting. Leadership development programs can cultivate essential soft skills, such as communication, emotional intelligence, and conflict resolution, crucial for effective management.

Additionally, workshops focusing on productivity and performance planning can empower managers to create strategic goals, align team efforts, and optimize workflow. Training in project management methodologies ensures managers possess the tools to lead and execute complex initiatives successfully. Continuous education in areas like organizational behavior, change management, and strategic planning equips managers with the insights and frameworks needed to navigate dynamic business environments. Overall, a well-rounded combination of formal education, specialized courses, and practical workshops contributes to a manager's proficiency in handling diverse challenges and fostering team success.

The Value of Lessons Learned by Accomplished Managers and Leaders

One of the most effective strategies for a manager to enhance effectiveness is to glean insights from the experiences of other successful managers and leaders. This type of learning proves effective because it offers real-world examples and practical lessons that transcend theoretical knowledge. By studying the journeys, decisions, and challenges faced by accomplished leaders, a manager gains a broader perspective on diverse leadership styles and strategies.

Learning from the successes and, equally importantly, the mistakes of others fosters a more informed and nuanced approach to decision-making. It allows managers to refine their own leadership style, adapt to different situations, and anticipate potential pitfalls. Additionally, this experiential learning from seasoned leaders helps managers navigate complex organizational dynamics, inspiring confidence and competence in their role.

What I find interesting about learning from the lessons of others is that, when it comes to some of the most accomplished business leaders in the world, a few common lessons emerge: purpose, integrity, work ethic, innovation, focus on the customer and results, and taking risks. Following are the most frequently mentioned lessons learned by several highly-regarded leaders:

ON MANAGEMENT

1. **Warren Buffett:** Focus on long-term investments, have a strong work ethic, be honest and transparent, and have a clear understanding of your business.

2. **Samuel Walton:** Believe in yourself and your idea, provide excellent customer service, and stay focused on your goals.

3. **John P. Morgan:** Have a strong sense of integrity, be willing to take calculated risks, and be willing to invest in the right people and ideas.

4. **Alfred Sloan:** Emphasize teamwork, delegate responsibilities, and be open to new ideas and approaches.

5. **Jack Welch:** Continuously innovate, embrace change, and focus on results.

6. **Steve Jobs:** Continuously innovate, challenge the status quo, and have a clear vision and sense of purpose.

7. **Walter A. Haas:** Emphasize teamwork, focus on the customer, and continuously innovate and improve.

8. **Indra Nooyi:** Focus on the customer, continuously innovate, and have a clear vision and sense of purpose.

9. **Arianna Huffington:** Emphasize work-life balance, focus on the customer, and continuously innovate and improve.

10. **Henry J. Heinz:** Emphasize quality, be transparent and honest, and focus on the needs of the customer.

Years ago, when I was a new, first-time manager, a corporate executive visiting offices in the region asked me a series of questions, and I couldn't answer them. It did not go over well. A valuable lesson I learned those many years ago is that every manager should always be prepared and confidently able to answer three questions:

1. What is the current status of the team/project/department/business unit, and what challenges are you facing?
2. What are your goals for the team/project/department/business unit, and how are you planning to achieve them?
3. How are you measuring success, and what metrics are you using to track progress?

These three questions help managers assess the current situation, set clear goals, and measure the impact of their decisions and actions. By being able to answer these questions, a manager can demonstrate their understanding of the team or department they are responsible for, their plans for the future, and their commitment to measuring and improving performance.

Answering these questions requires a manager to have a clear understanding of the current state of the team or department, as well as a vision for the future and a plan for how to get there. It also requires a manager to be knowledgeable about the metrics and data used to measure success and to use this information to make informed decisions and track progress over time. Managers who are unable to answer these questions with specifics and confidence risk lessening their credibility with their team, organizational leadership, and other relevant stakeholders.

Aspire to Leadership

Becoming a "leader" is a crucial evolution for managers, as it involves a shift in mindset and approach. While managers focus on efficiently managing tasks and resources, leaders inspire and guide their teams towards shared goals. The major differences lie in their perspectives: managers prioritize control and execution, whereas leaders focus on vision, inspiration, and influencing positive change.

To traverse the journey from manager to leader, certain activities play a pivotal role. Building trust and transparency forms the foundation, creating an environment where employees feel secure. Establishing credibility enhances influence and fosters respect, while genuine conversations and active listening demonstrate empathy and understanding. Following through on commitments and maintaining consistency builds reliability, instilling confidence in the team.

Respecting employees as adults, showing vulnerability, and treating them with openness and honesty contribute to a culture of trust and psychological safety. Understanding individual aspirations, helping employees achieve personal and professional goals, and recognizing their contributions strengthen the leader-employee relationship. Adopting a humble approach, avoiding surprises in feedback, and promoting a growth mindset that embraces failure all contribute to an empowering leadership style.

Ultimately, leaders trust their employees, appear confident, and in control—even when they are not—and consistently provide recognition for a job well done. Empowering employees when appropriate and ensuring open communication contribute to a positive work environment where individuals can thrive, marking the successful transition from manager to leader.

> **Leadership is achieving significant positive impact by building an organization of people working together on a common goal.**

Be Human: Laugh!

Transactional and humanistic manager-employee relationships represent two distinct approaches to the interaction between managers and their subordinates.

In a transactional manager-employee relationship, the focus is primarily on the exchange of resources and rewards. Managers set clear expectations for performance, and employees are motivated by tangible rewards such as salary increases, bonuses, or promotions. This approach relies on a structured framework of rules and regulations, and communication is often directive and task-oriented. The advantage of a transactional relationship lies in its clarity and simplicity. Employees know what is expected of them, and managers can easily measure performance against predetermined metrics. However, the downside is that it may lead to a lack of employee engagement and creativity, as the emphasis is primarily on compliance with established rules.

On the other hand, a humanistic manager-employee relationship centers around the well-being and personal development of employees. Managers adopting a humanistic approach prioritize open communication, collaboration, and understanding the individual needs of each team member. This approach recognizes the importance of intrinsic motivation, personal growth, and a positive work environment.

The pros of a humanistic relationship include higher employee satisfaction, increased creativity, and a sense of belonging within the organization. However, it may be challenging to measure success using traditional metrics, and the lack of clear guidelines can lead to ambiguity.

Relating as a humanistic manager can be more productive in fostering a positive workplace culture. When employees feel valued, supported, and empowered, they are more likely to be motivated and committed to their work. This can result in increased productivity, innovation, and a higher level of job satisfaction. Humanistic managers often build strong, collaborative teams that are resilient and adaptable to change. While it may require more effort in terms of communication and relationship-building, the long-term benefits of employee loyalty and a positive work environment outweigh the initial challenges.

An important yet little-discussed quality of good managers is *a sense of humor*. Laughter accelerates feelings of trust, closeness, and comfort. When people share a laugh, their brains release certain hormones—endorphins and dopamine—that emulate the feeling of a runner's high, a drug, or a brief state of extreme joy and delight. This chemical reaction in your brain is what makes you feel bonded with others. Following this logic, leaders who share a laugh with their employees can foster stronger connections with them. Their relationships can go from being "transactional" to human.

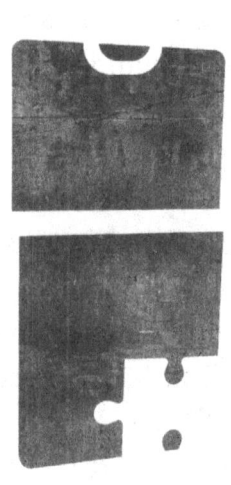

CONCLUSION

The Future Arrived Today

The future landscape for organizations is poised for significant changes driven by ongoing technological advancements, global trends, and shifts in workforce dynamics. Artificial intelligence, automation, and data analytics are expected to play increasingly pivotal roles in organizational operations, demanding that managers acquire digital literacy and the ability to harness these technologies effectively. Remote and flexible work arrangements, accelerated by recent events, will continue to reshape traditional workplace structures, necessitating managers to lead diverse and geographically dispersed teams adeptly.

In the future, the role of the manager is likely to evolve towards a more *strategic and collaborative* function. Managers will be expected to navigate complex, ambiguous situations, emphasizing creativity, critical thinking, and emotional intelligence. With the rise of remote work, fostering a positive organizational culture and maintaining team cohesion will be paramount. Adaptability and continuous learning will be essential for managers to stay ahead of industry changes, and the ability to lead through influence rather than authority will gain prominence.

CONCLUSION

Moreover, the future will demand an increased focus on ethical leadership, sustainability, and corporate social responsibility. Managers will need to integrate these values into their decision-making processes, aligning organizational goals with broader societal and environmental concerns. The emphasis on diversity, equity, and inclusion will intensify, requiring managers to champion inclusive practices and cultivate diverse talent.

As organizations grapple with a rapidly changing landscape, managers must embrace a proactive, agile mindset. The future manager will be a catalyst for innovation, a facilitator of collaboration, and a steward of organizational values, driving sustained success in a dynamic and interconnected world.

"On Management" has endeavored to be more than a mere guide; it aspires to be a steadfast companion for practicing managers in their journey toward excellence. Through a comprehensive exploration of management principles, practical insights, and thoughtful perspectives, this book seeks to equip managers with the tools needed to navigate the complexities of their roles effectively. The goal is not only to enhance current practices but to instill a mindset that embraces continuous learning and adaptation to the evolving landscape of management. As we turn the final page, my sincere hope is that readers find enduring value in these pages, making "On Management" a source of inspiration and guidance throughout their careers.

ABOUT THE AUTHOR

Tab Edwards is a principal with The Performance Laboratory No. 33, a business services consultancy and think tank that collaborates with business and organizational leaders to facilitate improved decision-making, translate those decisions into actionable plans, and achieve sustainable success. His principles have been embraced by organizations worldwide, and his best practices have been implemented by firms of various types, including global enterprises, corporations, SMBs, startups, public sector organizations, universities, and non-profits.

Edwards, the author of thirteen books, including a Bestseller, is a globally recognized consultant and critical thinker specializing in business-unit level strategy, leadership & management, performance improvement, productivity, and execution.

Before joining The Performance Lab, Edwards held global consulting and leadership positions at some of the world's most admired companies, including IBM Corporation, General Electric, AmerisourceBergen, The Water Group, and Hewlett-Packard.

He holds degrees from The University of Pittsburgh and the Pennsylvania State University, and initiated his doctoral studies at Pace University's Lubin School of Business.

THE BOOK'S COVER ART

A briefcase, as a symbol for a manager, embodies the essence of responsibility, organization, and preparedness. Much like a manager who carries the weight of decision-making, a briefcase holds the tools and documents necessary for the manager's daily tasks. It signifies the need for a manager to be well-prepared, capable of handling diverse challenges, and equipped with the essential resources to navigate the professional landscape.

The puzzle piece serves as a symbolic representation of a manager's role in the larger organizational picture. A manager is akin to a crucial puzzle piece, contributing a unique set of skills, perspectives, and responsibilities that interlock with those of their team and the organization. The puzzle piece emphasizes the idea that a manager is an integral part of a larger whole, with each piece playing a vital role in achieving organizational success. It conveys the interconnectedness and collaboration required for effective management within the broader context of the workplace puzzle. It also reflects a common vision, alignment, and the ability to solve problems.

All artwork has been created by The Lab Creative, a group within The Lab No 33 Media.

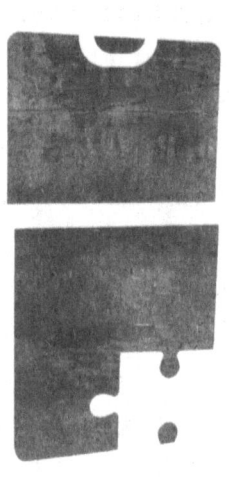

PROGRAMS

From The Performance Lab No 33

BUSINESS UNIT STRATEGY	PERFORMANCE IMPROVEMENT	MANAGEMENT & LEADERSHIP
Strategic Consulting	Performance Assessment	"On Management" Mgr. Performance Consulting
Strategic Planning Facilitation	Performance Consulting	"On Management" Mgr. Performance Coaching
Strategy Execution Support	Performance Improvement Workshops	New Manager School
Strategic Planning Workshops	Productivity Improvement	Performance Planning Workshops
Strategy & Planning Coaching and Consulting for Managers	Productivity Program Development	Performance Planning Coaching and Workshops
Strategy Keynote Addresses	Job Success Coaching, Consulting, and Workshops	Leadership Productivity and Coaching
MBI: Management By initiatives Workshop	Sales Optimization	Leadership Workshops
Strategy Alignment to the Performance Plan	Effective Communication and Presentation Skills	"On Management" Keynote Address

For more information, visit our website at www.TheLab33.com to download our services brochure. You can also contact our representatives at info@thelab33.com.

www.ingramcontent.com/pod-product-compliance
Lightning Source LLC
LaVergne TN
LVHW031616060526
838201LV00028B/321/J